Praise for *The Lost Coin: A Memoir of Adoption and Destiny*

"Dr. Stephen Rowley's *The Lost Coin: A Memoir of Adoption and Destiny* tells the story of the author's experience as an adopted child and his search for identity and belonging. What sets this book apart is the psychological perspective Rowley brings to the story, as he delves into the complex emotions and experiences that come with adoption—feelings of loss, identity confusion, and the search for oneself through the search for one's birth family. Rowley does a fantastic job of weaving together his personal narrative with depth psychological insights, making for a deep and thought-provoking read."

— Stacey Shelby, PhD, Depth Psychotherapist and author of *Love and Soul-Making: Searching the Depths of Romantic Love*

"An old Zen parable notes that we are all looking for the face we had before the world was made. Given up for adoption as an infant, Stephen Rowley, in *The Lost Coin,* depicts his multi-decade search for his roots and illustrates this profound drive for self-knowledge. His personal story touches on questions that rise for all of us as we explore the threads of history that brought us to this troubled present."

— James Hollis, PhD, Jungian Analyst and author of numerous books, most recently *The Broken Mirror: Refracted Visions of Ourselves*

"As a psychotherapist and an adoptee myself, I was deeply moved by Stephen Rowley's *The Lost Coin.* I could feel so well the immense pain involved in the process of separation and adoption, and touched by the reunion of the author and his biological mother. As Jung said, 'You can only take a client as far as you've gone yourself,' and by bringing us along on his journey, Rowley is able to share the wisdom he has gleaned. I highly recommend this book to anyone seeking to know more about relational complexities, and especially the complexities inherent to most, if not all adoptees."

— Shirin Fouladi Ruf, MA, LMFT, Psychotherapist, Stairway Recovery Center

"Every adoptee or anyone affiliated with adoption should read *The Lost Coin*. What a fascinating and insightful look into the journey of Stephen Rowley and the impact adoption has had on his life. This memoir delves into the root issue of '*Who Am I?*' that every adoptee struggles with, and the effects of separation from one's biological mother at birth."

— KelLee Parr, Author of *My Little Valentine: The Story of a Mother and Daughter's Lost Love* and *Mansion on a Hill: The Story of The Willows Maternity Sanitarium and the Adoption Hub of America.*

"Dr. Stephen Rowley's book about his journey is a must-read for adoptees and professionals who work in the field of adoption. Steve's first letter to me was very well-written from the adoptee's point of view and grabbed me as a genuine request to complete himself and find the 'missing coin.' I knew from my first contact with him that he was on a mission. I had received lots of letters from adoptees before, but there was something different about his request. He was on a journey to find out about his history and wasn't going to stop until that was accomplished. Steve's story of his journey to get his biological history and make the emotional connection with his birth family is well-documented and worth the time to read."

— Tom X. Lazio, Former Executive Director of American Home Finding Association, Ottumwa, Iowa

"From my own experience as a late-discovery adoptee in reunion and as a professional coach with over 20 years of experience guiding adults navigating midlife transitions, searching for answers to the question, *Who am I?,* is an experience every human being will encounter at some point in their lives. Dr. Stephen Rowley's memoir, *The Lost Coin*, is not only a poignant description of his inner experience of being an adoptee who literally embarks on a decades-long search for the answer to this question, but Dr. Rowley also opens our eyes to consider a universal message for any of us struggling in navigating the unknown. That is, the invisible and powerful force that destiny plays in our lifelong search for wholeness and healing. His experience illustrates that when we are ready and willing to open ourselves up to see the hidden meaning and truths behind our own losses and struggles, we will come to know their purpose for our unique path to growth and healing."

— Nancy McCaughey, Principal and Professional Certified Coach, Nancy McCaughey Coaching, LLC

"I am pleased to recommend Stephen Rowley's book, *The Lost Coin*, as a heartfelt account of the story of adoption. It is especially relevant for those who have been impacted by adoption – those who have been adopted, those who have adopted or are considering it, and others who want to know more. With his background as a psychotherapist and educator, his interest in Jungian psychology and the Eastern philosophy of the lamas, he brings insight into the inner life of those who have been adopted and how others can better understand this journey."

— Janet Tatum, MSW, Jungian Analyst, PNSJA/IAAP, Certified Sandplay Therapist – Teaching Member STA/ISST, Philemon Foundation Board Member, Redmond, Washington

The Lost Coin: A Memoir of Adoption and Destiny details the long and at times painful passage of the adoptee to understand their feelings, their past, and to go on living, gaining the feeling of being real in a family that does not share genetic inheritance. Stephen Rowley's quest to differentiate his feelings and to validate and believe what he felt, hence grounding himself in his emotional life while accepting and loving himself for the child he had been, is the journey of the adoptee."

—Audrey Punnett, PhD, RPT-S, CST-T, Jungian Child, Adolescent & Adult Analyst (IAAP), author of *The Orphan: A Journey to Wholeness,* and coauthor of *Jungian Child Analysis.* She is a graduate of the C.G. Jung Institute, Zurich, and an Associate Clinical Professor of Psychiatry at the University of California San Francisco Fresno.

"In *The Lost Coin,* Dr. Stephen Rowley eloquently shares his journey of searching for his birth parents. While he underscores the lifelong impact of the trauma of separation of child from parent, he also helps us all to understand the human spirit that both craves and relentlessly reaches for self, hope, and grace. This compellingly honest book will be a comfort for those who are part of an adoption journey and may still be searching for healing, and an incredibly useful witness for those standing ready to help."

— Rita Soronen, President & CEO, Dave Thomas Foundation for Adoption

THE
LOST
COIN

A Memoir of
Adoption and Destiny

Stephen Rowley

CHIRON PUBLICATIONS • ASHEVILLE, NORTH CAROLINA

www.ChironPublications.com

Cover photo by strelok (Dzianis Miraniuk)/depositphotos.com
Interior and cover design by Danijela Mijailovic.
Printed primarily in the United States of America.

ISBN 978-1-68503-175-6 paperback
ISBN 978-1-68503-176-3 hardcover
ISBN 978-1-68503-177-0 electronic
ISBN 978-1-68503-178-7 limited edition paperback

Library of Congress Cataloging-in-Publication Data Pending

To Robert Galloway,

like the red wheelbarrow,

on whom so much depends.

CONTENT'S

AUTHOR'S NOTE

I wrote this book to share my life's quest to answer one question: *Who am I?* The mysteries of my adoption and the lack of clarity about my identity led me to search for my birth parents for sixty years. This is the true story of the people, events, and twists of fate that shaped my search and me. I've included the real names of members of my family, as well as some friends, colleagues, and public figures. However, I changed the names and locations of my birth parents, their families, and a few others out of respect for their well-deserved privacy.

A Story That Could Be True
William Stafford

If you were exchanged in the cradle and
your real mother died
without ever telling the story
then no one knows your name,
and somewhere in the world
your father is lost and needs you
but you are far away.

He can never find
how true you are, how ready.
When the great wind comes
and the robberies of the rain
you stand on the corner shivering.
The people who go by –
you wonder at their calm.

They miss the whisper that runs
any day in your mind,
"Who are you really, wanderer?" –
and the answer you have to give
no matter how dark and cold
the world around you is:
"Maybe I'm a king."

INTRODUCTION

Be patient toward all that is unsolved in your heart and try to
love the questions themselves, like locked rooms and like books
that are now written in a very foreign tongue. Do not now seek
the answers, which cannot be given you because you would not
be able to live them. And the point is, to live everything. Live the
questions now. Perhaps you will then gradually, without noticing
it, live along some distant day into the answer.
~ Rainer Maria Rilke, Austrian poet ~

At my twentieth high school reunion, a former classmate approached me with a look that made me think I should remember
him. I didn't, until I saw the yearbook photo on his name tag.
Before he uttered a word, I played it off, "Hey Charles! How you
doin' man? Long time, no see!"

I was surprised that he'd recognized me, as my looks
hardly matched the photo on my name badge. While I still had
dark hair, it was much longer now, with wisps of gray. I had a dark
mustache and styled hair, which my then-girlfriend (and later wife)
thought made me look like Tom Selleck of the original *Magnum,
P.I.* I fancied that I looked the part of West Coast success. In the
past 20 years, I had been a campus radical, one-time-only drug
dealer, hospital orderly, received a PhD from Stanford, run two
marathons, traveled Europe, taught school and been a principal—
and a would-be Buddhist. I vaguely remembered that Charles
owned a barbershop in town. I had left in 1967 to go to college
and never looked back. Charles, on the other hand, never left.

What Charles saw in me, I surmised, was a reflection of my former high school self: Mr. Bigshot. I was surrounded by old friends, standing confidently with a drink in my hand, past girlfriends and old football buddies at my side. Once more, I was at the hub of a smart and popular circle of friends. Charles and I rarely crossed paths in high school. We had nothing in common. We knew nothing of each other.

As he drew closer in the dimly lit ballroom, he looked me straight in the eye and spoke with a soft, familiar Iowa drawl. "Well, Steve…I've known you thirty years and you haven't changed a bit. You betcha. There you go. Good to see you, man." Then with a quick handshake, he slipped back to his corner of the ballroom like a phantom fading into mist. As he departed, I blurted out, "Well, *I'm doing what I can.*" But he didn't hear me. He was gone.

At first, I took his comment as a compliment. He wasn't trying to be rude or condescending. He was just calling it the way he saw it, like a baseball umpire, and I respected his honesty. But his words left me unsettled, as though he'd seen through me. I felt oddly vulnerable and out of place. Despite the half-drunken revelry with my coterie of friends, I suddenly felt alone, a feeling I was all too familiar with.

Even after the reunion, Charles's words continued to haunt me. What did he mean I hadn't changed? That was a stupid thing to say. I was a grown man, not a senior in high school. I'd done a lot and had the résumé to prove it. *What did he know about me anyway?* Maybe he wanted to take me down a notch or two. I had moved on with my life, perhaps forgetting where I had come from? Was that how my other classmates saw me too?

None of them knew much about me, and no one knew the deeper reason I'd returned to town that week. Yes, I looked forward to seeing old friends and hearing exaggerated tales of our rowdy times in the Sixties. The intoxicating dance of flirtation with old flames also needed tending. But these weren't enough to bring me home. Few at the reunion knew I had been adopted. None could have guessed that in a few days, I'd be driving to a small town on the other side of Iowa, trying to find information about the young woman who gave birth to me at a home for unwed mothers. They assumed that I was the natural son of my successful parents, who'd raised me in a beautiful home across from the country club. But I was actually the illegitimate son of a young woman who gave me up at birth.

Even after years of looking, I had no idea that I was on the cusp of a discovery that would change my life and the lives of others. I could not have guessed that in the coming year, I would find her in circumstances that would break my heart. This would be one more turn in my life's journey to discover my identity. That night, hanging out with old friends was enough. Still, I was unnerved by Charles's statement. Had I really not changed in thirty years? *Who was I?*

I often wonder whether other adoptees share the deep-seated drive to discover their birth parents that I felt from the day Mom and Dad told me I'd been adopted. Do other adoptees obsess about their identities and the circumstances of their adoption? By what forces of nature, or fate, does anyone become who they are? These are the questions of philosophers, analysts, astrologers, and seekers. These are the questions that have framed my life.

Beyond the details of my biological ancestry, I became curious about the long-term psychological impact of adoption. This memoir is a part of that exploration—the interplay of inner and outer, and the steps along the way. In writing about my own life, I hope to give voice and encouragement to other adoptees, long silenced and frustrated by laws and protocols that have kept this information from us.

I am now a depth psychotherapist, and I wrote this book as a *personal myth*, an individual's story for making sense and meaning of the world. My own telling is woven together by personal and professional strands of imagination, intuition, and life experience. As Rilke wrote, I am *living my questions*, and perhaps someday without noticing, I will have lived into the answers.

PART ONE

In all of us there is a hunger, marrow deep,
to know our heritage,
to know who we are, and where we have come from.
Without this enriching knowledge, there is hollow yearning;
no matter what our attainments in life,
there is the most disquieting loneliness.[1]
~ Alex Haley, American writer ~

1. Who Am I?

I was adopted as a young child. That fact set the trajectory of my life, and I've spent my whole life trying to discover who I am. Growing up, I didn't know my original name, who my parents were, or the circumstances of my adoption. These were hidden from me, mostly the result of state adoption regulations and codes of privacy that protect those who have given up children for adoption. In labor and environmental law, there is a "right to know." But in the case of adoption, the curiosity and drive to uncover one's identity are often not welcome. As a result, to this day I guard my independence ferociously, and mistrust rules and bureaucracies.

I was adopted when I was six months old by a highly respectable Midwestern couple. From the start, they told me I was adopted. My mother would say, "You *are* special and so lucky! We *chose* you! That doesn't happen to other boys and girls. We wanted you and you made us happy from the moment we brought you home." Her words sounded reassuring, but eventually I began to wonder what they thought of my three siblings—two brothers and a sister born to them after I was adopted. Weren't they special too? I was just a kid, trying to make sense of it all.

My parents were affluent by Midwestern standards and I grew up in a loving home, yet I never shed the *feeling* of being an orphan. I was popular as a kid and did well in school and sports. I was destined for success, they said, but on the inside, I felt utterly alone. I hid the feeling of disconnection and my desire to know more. Most adoptees, I believe, know this paradox—having it all yet feeling empty on the inside, longing for community. I tried to simply accept my parents' version of being chosen.

Dr. and Mrs. Robert Rowley found me at an adoption agency in Ottumwa, Iowa in 1949. They told the story as if they were shopping in a department store. I was the size, shape and color they were looking for. They could have picked other babies, but they chose me. Friends and relatives would remark how much I looked like my dad, with brown hair and brown eyes like his. Maybe that's why they selected me—like father, like son. I never thought twice about my parents' description of it all.

When I was twelve, they showed me my birth certificate. It said I was born in Kansas City, Missouri—not Ottumwa, Iowa— on February 10, 1949, with Robert and Ruth Rowley listed as my parents. Time of birth was blank. I wondered if I had a different name before I became Stephen Robert Rowley? Until the day my curiosity began to blaze, I kept this question and others like it to myself.

I was an only child until five, when my brother was born. Mostly what I remember from those years was being privileged— not spoiled but the center of attention. I was even-tempered and well-mannered. I picked up my books and toys, didn't whine when it was time to go to bed, and was easily bribed with food to behave. I was rarely spanked, and was the apple of everyone's eye. Actually, I don't even remember much of that. This was my mother's telling and I have no reason to doubt it.

Our white, two-story house in Burlington, Iowa seemed huge to me. I had plenty of picture books and play things, including an array of cowboy hats, toy six-shooters and rifles, and a rocking horse that looked like Roy Rogers' Trigger. It didn't take long for Mom to realize that our round-screen Zenith TV was a cheap and reliable babysitter, which initiated my cultural programming with shows like *Ding Dong School,* a precursor to *Sesame Street,* and *The Howdy Doody Show* with Buffalo Bob and Clarabell the Clown. Today I realize that millions of us Baby Boomers were watching the same shows, being programmed by TV programs.

Mom bought me a lot of records, the music and stories propelling me into the magical world of imagination. She would throw a blanket over a card table, transforming it into a tent, cave, or rocket-ship capsule. I would crawl underneath and listen to records for hours, on adventures in the jungle, journeys into outer space, and encounters as a cowboy in the Old West.

I also have hazy images of picnics, fishing on a pond with Dad, riding my pony, Star, on Grandma and Grandpa's farm, and going to Sunday School, the one thing I was really not crazy about. Dressing up on Easter Sunday was the worst. There is a picture of me dutifully outfitted in a white starched shirt, bowtie, shiny black shoes, and a short gray wool overcoat with the bob of a navy-blue hat tilted back on my head. My, I was cute, with my hair slathered with Brylcreem. I rather liked the scent, but my discomfort of being dolled up was the beginning of not liking church.

Then at five, my world was interrupted by another child in the house. My baby brother had a heart condition, which worried my parents. He was colicky and his incessant squalling disrupted the tranquility of my world. I didn't like it but I kept my mouth shut. Mom looked worried all the time, and I didn't want my complaints to add to it.

Soon after my brother's birth, we moved to Iowa City so my father could complete his surgical residency at the University of Iowa Hospitals. Gone was our big white house, replaced by a small two-bedroom house with a flat roof and yard barely big enough for a swing set. The new neighborhood seemed normal, but my mom was bothered that the next door neighbors were Catholic—and had six kids. I found it strange that they didn't eat meat on Fridays and there were pictures of Jesus on a cross all over their house, but I just didn't understand what the problem was. They did have to go to church before sunrise on Sundays, and for that reason alone I was glad we weren't Catholic.

Two neighborhood boys took me on as their little brother, including me in their pickup football games and basement clubhouse, which we entered through a trap door. I got to help them selling candy and cold pop and parking cars on our lawns on Saturdays when the Hawkeyes played just four blocks away. We split the profits and bought real football helmets with matching jerseys. I was in heaven.

Dad was often on-call, spending nights at the hospital on thirty-six-hour shifts. Mom shouldered the household duties raising my brother, our new baby sister, and me. The younger kids would fight and fuss all day long, driving Mom crazy and me too. To escape the racket at home, I played outside with the neighbor kids as late as I could. When I couldn't go out, Mom kept me busy with books from the library and workbooks she had sent away for. I loved the downtown library's reading program, especially in summer. I dove into the arithmetic and phonics workbooks, they were fun. When I got tired of the stuff that was supposed to make me smarter, I was allowed to watch *Popeye* and *Merry Melodies* cartoons on TV. Later, when *Three Stooges* reruns became the rage, Mom tried to ban my watching "those stupid men," but it was too little, too late. I was hooked for life.

I went to Roosevelt Elementary School, south of the University of Iowa campus. Our neighborhood was teeming with school-age Boomers back when adults (in neighborhoods like ours) didn't worry about their kids' whereabouts; someone always knew where we were. They didn't even care if we stayed out after dark as long as they could hear us. My world was like the popular TV show of the time *The Adventures of Ozzie and Harriet*, and my dream was to be like Rickie Nelson singing "Travelin' Man" or another song at the end of each episode.

There were no Black people in our neighborhood until my parents sold our house to a Black physician from the University Hospital in 1958. Before closing the deal, Dad checked with the neighbors to see if there were any objections to having a "Negro" family next door. Negro was the polite term used back then to refer to Black people. We kids in white Midwestern towns were oblivious to racial issues. Schools and textbooks never mentioned discrimination, segregation, or even slavery; and race was not a topic of conversation at our dinner tables. Our minds were whitewashed—covered over by layers of denial, ignorance, and implicit racism. Our parents held tightly to a life free of diversity. To get along, we went along. Later, as I discovered the world outside my white Iowa neighborhoods, the patina of Midwestern homogeneity shattered, never to be as it once was to me.

2. My First Glimpse – Race and Poverty

My first memory of seeing people of color outside of sports was a trip with my grandfather to Chicago when I was seven. He brought me with him in the cab of a large cattle truck headed to the Chicago Stockyards. For five hours I sat scrunched between Grandpa and the driver, a mean-looking guy who smoked cigarettes, a habit my family held in contempt. But I forgot about the smoky ride when we arrived at the stockyards. Thousands of cattle and hogs were corralled in a maze of pens and fences, then routed into a long, narrow gateway. The animals were electrically prodded into to a low-ceilinged building where they were slaughtered, skinned, and put on a conveyor belt for butchering. Their anxious bellowing and squealing hung in the air, and the stench was awful. I was glad to get out of there.

As repulsive as the stockyard scene had been, it was not enough to prevent Grandpa and me from eating a big lunch at the Stock Yard Inn Dining Room, selecting from a menu of pork chops, meatloaf, mashed potatoes, corn on the cob, green beans with melted Velveeta cheese, homemade biscuits with gravy, sliced white bread with real butter, ice tea or milk, and soft vanilla ice cream. I feasted on a little of everything, a foodie in the making. Then Grandpa took me on the El, the elevated rail system, to see his beloved Cubs play at Wrigley Field.

I had never seen anything like Chicago, and I certainly hadn't seen inner-city poverty like I saw that day. As our smoke-filled train snaked past the narrow corridors of indistinguishable tenement buildings, my seven-year-old eyes bugged out in shock. Tiers of threadbare laundry hung over lines of frayed rope stretched between buildings. Rusty dumpsters cluttered darkened alleys. The deep lumbering groan of the train's engine mixed with the rhythmic clank of its steel wheels in a monstrous roar that ricocheted off the walls and back through the open windows of our train car. As we made our way to the North Side of Chicago, everyone I saw in apartment windows, doorways, and on the sidewalks was Black. If I had held any expectations of coming to Chicago, it would have been of Eliot Ness, Al Capone, and gangsters, not the slums I saw that day.

The moment we entered Wrigley Field, thoughts of the tenements, the El, and Al Capone vanished. The rich green outfield grass, red infield clay, starched white bases, and brilliant, cloudless blue sky hanging above a darkened Lake Michigan exploded before my eyes. Just twenty rows behind third base sat Grandpa—an old farmer in a plaid shirt and straw hat—and me, a sturdy-looking seven-year-old in a striped T-shirt and blue jeans, taking in the day. I'll remember that moment with him always. It was splendid. Even at seven, I knew how special it was to see the great Ernie Banks play ball—in person!

Memories of that weekend are with me today, including my uneasy mix of emotions. On one hand was the adventure with Ernie Banks, Wrigley Field, and lunch at the Stock Yard Inn. And on the other, the sea of farm animals being led to slaughter and the panorama of poverty that left me reeling, confused, and even embarrassed by it all. It was a roller coaster ride of excitement and despair. I left that day feeling a little more grown up, although unsure I liked the feeling. I never told any of this to Grandpa, as I don't think he would have understood. I was alone with a sense that the sheen of my innocence had been tarnished, the bubble of my bucolic boyhood burst.

Late that afternoon we boarded the Denver Zephyr passenger train to go home. The Cubs had won the game, but I felt strangely sad processing all I had seen. I knew something important had happened, but I had no words for it. My grandfather was a stoic man whose leathered skin, calloused hands, and stooped shoulders told a silent story of the hard life of a farmer. Even then I knew he looked tired, and older than he should. He had withstood the staggering deprivations of the Great Depression, the wild fluctuations of weather and crop prices, and the fear of losing a son in war. But unlike most farm couples, he and Grandma were determined to see their children escape the confines of rural life by getting a good education. Their daughter, my Auntie Kathryn, became a teacher and their son, my dad, became a doctor.

My main comfort on that train ride home was the piney scent of my souvenir baseball. My tired head resting on the train car window, I stared at the rows of corn flickering by. Then the bright orange sun sank beneath the horizon as night descended. As the dim overhead train lights clicked on above our heads, I held my new baseball close to my nose, then brushed my cheek with its ruby red stitching, back-and-forth. Wow! I had been to Wrigley

Field. Half way home, I glanced up at Grandpa and saw him gently snoring, his grizzled chin bobbing up and down. He looked so worn out. But I loved sitting next to him, as the rhythmic cadence of the train wheels clacked through the night.

When we arrived in Monmouth later that night, Grandma and Auntie Kathryn greeted us with a thermos of coffee for Grandpa and a small pack of cookies for me, and drove us back to the farm. "How was it?" they asked. "What did you do? What did you see?"

"Oh!" I exclaimed, though half asleep. "I ate pork chops and saw Ernie Banks! And look at my new baseball!" I knew that would make them happy.

I nestled up against Auntie Kathryn in the plush back seat of their old Hudson as we headed down the narrow highway toward the gravel road that would take us to the farm. I tucked my baseball under my jacket and held it closely. I thought of the cows, the El, and especially of the Black people in those big apartment buildings. It was almost midnight. I must have fallen right to sleep, as the next thing I heard was the sound of Grandpa cooking eggs in a large cast iron skillet. From my small single bed upstairs, I could already smell bacon and eggs frying in grease.

I enjoyed one more glorious summer with Grandma, Grandpa and Auntie Kathryn. Grandpa took me to Chicago again, this time to see the White Sox with Nellie Fox and Luis Aparicio. We also took long road trips with Grandma and Auntie Kathryn to Baltimore, Washington, D.C., New York City, Niagara Falls, Lake Erie, and Cleveland—four of which had major league baseball teams! Their new two-toned Nash Rambler was fancier than the Hudson. It had push-button gears and a modern-looking radio, which they rarely used. I don't think we fooled anybody, though. We still looked like country hicks in the big cities. In New York, Grandpa drove north on Columbus Avenue, almost to Harlem. We eventually stopped at a dreary looking hotel where an elderly doorman opened the car door for Grandma. He didn't say much to us, especially after Grandpa forgot to tip him.

Macy's was our first stop. I was eight, and I spent an hour going up and down the escalators on my own. After Macy's, we headed to the nearest Horn and Hardart Automat for lunch. The food on display behind small glass doors was ready to eat— perhaps an early prototype for Amazon Fresh. The Automat was the neatest thing ever—even better than waitresses on roller skates at the drive-in back home.

Summers on the Rowley farm were like a dream. Grandma and Grandpa gave me a lot of independence, even allowing me to drive the rusty red Farmall tractor alongside the barn by myself. But in a blink of an eye, I awoke from that dream and never spent another summer on my grandparents' farm.

3. Witness to Heartache

My dad finished his residency in the spring of 1958 and we moved back to Burlington, just in time for Little League tryouts. I was big and strong for my age, and I was quickly selected by a really good team. My fielding was mediocre, but I could hit home runs, which meant a lot to the team and me. I stopped spending summers slopping hogs back on the farm and pursued the glories of baseball.

Earlier that year, an unexpected rift had opened between my grandparents and Auntie Kathryn. To me, she was the best playmate a boy could have had. She was always at the farm in summers while on vacation from her job as a biology teacher in town. In the community, though, she was known as a spinster— shy, dour, and a woman who could flash her fiery temper before you even saw it coming. She put the fear of God into her students at Monmouth High and would scare the bejesus out of anyone in our family when she was on a tear. Fortunately, I almost always got a pass from her rants and sharp tongue. We were close whenever we were alone, and I was proud to be her favorite.

During my last summer at the farm, Kathryn was dating a man, perhaps for the first time. He was close to her age of forty. She took me to see him play softball under the lights, and I liked him. He soon gave her a small diamond ring and they planned to announce their engagement. But at the last moment Grandpa stepped in and told her that the man she wanted to marry was not good enough for her or the Rowley family.

The sin her fiancé had committed was owning a small farm on "bottomland," which means land near a river or creek-bed with silty, sandy, less fertile soil. Bottomland was known to flood, and its soil could stay muddy well past planting season. Living in bottomland in the country was like living on the other side of the tracks in town. No bottomland people belonged to the Belmont Country Church that the Rowleys and their neighbors attended. Bottomland children did not attend the one-room schoolhouse next to the church, either. Bottomland people had no social standing and no future. Grandma's cousin, Loren Murphy, had been Chief Justice of the Illinois Supreme Court. Marrying a man of little means and low status would never do. What would people say?

Auntie Kathryn never whispered a word of this sad story to me, even later in her life. I got it from Mom. But soon after Kathryn's marriage plans were wrecked, she became unhinged. At Christmas gatherings, birthdays, and family get-togethers after that, she would routinely explode in anger or erupt in tears. At one Thanksgiving at the farm, with the whole family present, she had a meltdown over some misconstrued insult, ran out of the house without a coat, and drove her car pell-mell into a muddy field where it got stuck and she sat motionless. We could hear her crying inside her car even with the windows rolled up. My dad dutifully traipsed out to "settle her down." Eventually she came back to the house, but stayed in the basement for a long time before running upstairs to her room without a word. This episode and others like it scared the hell out of me. I was too young to understand the torment and shame that haunted her. This was my first encounter

18

with mental illness, and I cannot forget how unfairly she was treated by my grandparents or how she punished herself by living as a miserly hermit the rest of her life. The heartache and tragedy of dear Auntie Kathryn still lingers in my heart.

After her death in 2009, my siblings—David, Sue, and Bill—and I readied her house in Monmouth for sale. We packed up everything in one long day. Some things we just dumped or gave away, and we stored many of her precious antiques for auction in the spring. As my sister Sue opened one old dress box, she gasped aloud, "Oh, my God! What is this?" It was the moldy remnants of a white sheet cake with the words "Congratulations" and "Anniversary" barely legible in blue frosting lettering on top. I recognized it as the cake my parents bought for my grandparents' 50th wedding anniversary—forty years earlier. And now this desiccated cake-like object was a strange and poignant reminder that her parents had prevented the one chance she had to be happy. Yet she remained loyal to them to the end. In light of her devastating heartache, I will never understand why.

We also discovered two chests of drawers crammed with every Christmas or birthday gift ever given her. Some were still in their original wrapping and never opened. It was a pitiable sight, a remembrance of her self-inflicted deprivation.

In 2008, while Kathryn lingered in a nursing home, Mom (with her power of attorney) and I went to open her safe deposit box at a local bank, and were shocked to find a couple of hundred thousand dollars-worth of savings bonds and Treasury Bills, which she'd begun buying in the early 1950s—stacks of them bundled in order of date of purchase. She had spent next to nothing of her earnings on herself, often eating food from tin cans warmed on a hot plate. In winter, she kept her house just warm enough to keep the pipes from freezing and wore heavy coats indoors. But it was now obvious that she was rich enough to provide any comfort she could have desired, even secretly.

As Mom and I burrowed to the bottom of the safe deposit box, we found a small envelope with a lock of hair and her diamond wedding ring. We looked at each other, and in a rare but touching moment, we teared up, pushed the safe deposit box aside, and sat for a few moments in silence. This was one of the rare and glorious moments I shared with my mother. I think we may each have prayed for forgiveness for any unkind thoughts we'd ever had about Kathryn. If we didn't, we should have.

If it weren't for Auntie Kathryn, I might not have become a teacher two decades later. It pleased her a great deal when I did. But when I became a principal, I detected that look from her that spelled trouble. Miss Rowley rarely saw eye-to-eye with her high school principals. "There's no need for principals," she would often exclaim in a huff. "They just do what the school board tells them to do. No brains and no spine!" I pitied them. Miss Kathryn Rowley was a force of nature not be messed with.

4. Lucky Boy

By summer's end in 1958, I had completed my first year of Little League and entered the fourth grade in Sunnyside Elementary School in Burlington, Iowa—a mid-sized town of 25,000 on the banks of the Mississippi River. I made friends easily enough but Sunnyside was not as rigorous as Roosevelt Elementary School in Iowa City. At Roosevelt, many kids' parents had been university people. It seemed natural that we were expected to work diligently, speak up in class, and extend our reading through the town library program. Sunnyside was easier and I was soon bored. I tried pretending to look interested, but I was actually studying the teacher to see what she was would do next.

Most days I rode my bike home for lunch, which was nearly always a hot dog or peanut butter and jelly sandwich with Campbell's Soup. At noon each day, Paul Harvey's mellifluous baritone voice came on the radio with, "Hello, Americans. This is Paul Harvey. Stand by for news!" with his patented "and now for rest of the story..." and his boisterous staccato sign-off: "Good Day!!" Daily, he prattled a string of corny morality tales, quirky small town vignettes, and blatant advertising pitches, poorly disguised as genuine news. Paul Harvey was the voice of the postwar middle class all across Middle America. He was a constant presence in the Rowley household at lunch, Monday through Friday, without fail.

I experienced another kind of uneasiness in Burlington. While most kids lived in modest houses, we moved into a large two-story home on *Bittersweet Place* (honestly), surrounded by several acres of lawn and a hedge of orange-berried bittersweet. It prominently sat across a private lane from a country club. There was a large screened-in porch near the entrance and a sleeping porch on the second floor above it, along with servants' quarters that my dad used instead as his den. He kept the den under lock and key, storing his large collection of shotguns, pistols, high-powered rifles, derringers and ammunition there. I'm still fond of the sweet scent of Hoppe's gun oil that perfumed that part of the house.

Originally built as a summer home in the countryside a little outside Burlington, the property had a fenced-in apple orchard and once boasted a swimming pool, which had long been buried under a cluster of fir trees. To a passersby, it must have looked like a mansion. My parents bought it for $32,500—expensive in those days! Mom and Dad always drove nice cars—mostly Buicks except for the beat up Chevy Suburban Dad used for hunting trips and the bright red Mercury wagon for Mom's endless family chauffeuring.

My father was already a well-known doctor in Burlington, and he quickly established his new practice. Now that he didn't have to be on-call as much, he was freer to pursue his passions of hunting, fishing and flying. He owned and flew a series of planes while I grew up. He went big-game hunting in Montana and British Columbia. I never went with him on those trips, as they overlapped with football season. But I did go with the family on long summer vacations to places like Yellowstone and Glacier National Parks. We even drove to the World's Fair in Seattle in 1962, with a trailer hitched on the back of our station wagon. I could not have guessed that Seattle would eventually be my home.

It didn't take long for my teacher to see that I was far ahead of my classmates, and she suggested to my parents that I skip a year and enter the sixth grade. I resisted, as I didn't want to appear even more privileged, so I remained with kids my own age. This turned out to be an advantage in sports. At age twelve, I shed my husky blue jeans and shot up in height. At the All-City track meet, I won first place in the hundred-yard dash for sixth graders, and my love of running set in. I went on to excel in football, basketball, track, and tennis in high school.

By thirteen I was six-feet tall and possessed an athletic ability that others in my family didn't have. My interest in girls and active social life was nothing like my family, either. I was different on the outside now, just as I had always been on the inside.

5. Awakening to Loneliness

As my academic and athletic skills began to flourish, my self-consciousness also grew. I didn't want anyone to think we were rich. I knew from my parents that to see real wealth you had to go to Chicago. At Marshall Field's you could rub shoulders with people who had real money—the ones who lived in high-rise apartments and stone mansions on the North Shore of Lake Michigan. We were always small-town folks, content with roasting hot dogs and marshmallows on weekend picnics.

Still, during my elementary school years I became more aware of class differences. We lived in a big, beautiful home. Our cars were nicer and our clothes were never out of style or worn, and I felt uncomfortable knowing that others kids did not have the advantages I did. I was also keenly aware that I had been adopted into an affluent family—like winning the lottery, just a case of dumb luck.

Dad's parents were both from large farm families in western Illinois. Mom's dad had been a carpenter in Knoxville, Illinois, a small town near Galesburg. Her mother died soon after she graduated from high school, but she never said a word about her loss. My parents considered themselves down-to-earth people— no "puttin' on airs." The Great Depression was like yesterday to them, even though they rarely talked about it. My dad never talked about his time in the Navy in World War II, serving as a young MD and officer in the Pacific Theater. Those tumultuous events, however, cast a lasting shadow over their era—a generation that TV news anchor Tom Brokaw would later call "the Greatest Generation."

Both my parents grew up with little money, though neither considered themselves poor. But scarcity had had an enduring impact on them, and they remained frugal into adulthood, teaching my siblings and me to be the same. Every now and then, my mother would announce she'd be serving a Depression supper that night, featuring powdered milk (instead of real milk) and underbaked slices of eggplant she tried to convince us was meat. Or she'd remind us how lucky her family had been to have liver in the Depression years, and she would serve us liver and onions with gravy, calling it a real treat. I found it so awful that I comically protested, "If all the meat that people ate in the Depression was eggplant and liver and onions, no wonder they jumped out of buildings!" I was half-serious.

There was one dish my Swedish-heritage mom served on only one occasion that was worse than liver and onions—*lutefisk*, made from salted cod cured in lye, which became gelatinous after being rehydrated for days—traditionally part of a Scandinavian

Christmas. It was so putrid that no one would eat it. I'm surprised the neighbors didn't call the police about the smell!

I had friends whose dads were lawyers, bankers, and doctors. They lived in big houses, too. Some were large Victorians that sat on the high bluffs overlooking the Mississippi River. But most of the kids I went to school with were from middle- or working-class families. No nice cars, interesting vacations, and weekend rides in a Piper Comanche like me. Fortunately, the kids at my school were not especially class-conscious. No one paid much attention to kids who wore hand-me-downs or got new shoes only when the ones they wore every day fell apart.

Regardless of class, every kid I knew went to Sunday School at one church or another. For me, it was the First United Methodist Church downtown. My parents regularly attended, so it was expected that I would go to Sunday School there, Vacation Bible School, and be a part of the Youth Group. But I was at odds with religion from the start. I thought our Sunday School teachers were phony. The morality tales about leading a clean life like Jesus made no sense to me. No one ever tried to explain who or what God was, or why we were saved because Jesus was crucified. I still don't get it. The idea that we were born sinners was just too much for me, as were the hymns we had to sing. Sunday School felt like brainwashing.

In those days, a job at the local Case Tractor factory or the Iowa Army Ammunition Plant paid decent wages, and a worker could afford to buy a small house for his family and live a comfortable life. Dropping out of school to take a job at one of the many factories in Burlington was not a bad deal for the kids who would never go college. By the time I graduated from high school, though, blue collar wages had declined and the kids who didn't go on to college were just out of luck.

It was worse for Black families. To my knowledge, few factories in the post-war years in towns like Burlington hired Blacks for skilled trade jobs—only for unskilled work. Black people in our town lived on the "South End." There was de facto segregation at work, church, social circles, and even at school. Only two of the elementary schools in town had children of color. I don't remember any Black students in my college-track classes in high school. Sports was a different matter. Black and white kids played well together on teams. I cannot remember hearing racial epithets aimed at Black kids from their teammates and coaches, but I did hear racist taunts from adults directed at Black players from a few parents and others adults in the stands, and it made me ashamed and angry.

That said, we did not hang out after practice or go to each other's homes. It was unthinkable that a white boy would date a Black girl or that a Black girl would ask a white boy to a Sadie Hawkins dance. At the same time, none of us thought we were racist. Some of us were huge fans of Cassius Clay, and even more so when he became Muhammad Ali. We rooted for many cherished Black athletes. I even got to shake Jesse Owens' hand at a Methodist Church dinner in his honor. Of course, we assumed our affinity for Black athletes exempted us from the kind of racism we thought existed only in the South.

Regarding LGBTQ+ issues, no one I knew had even heard the term *homosexual*, talked about it, or understood it. Most (straight) adults either turned a blind eye or held deep, unexpressed fears and prejudices about it. Years later, I learned from gay friends how hidden and dangerous the gay underground of Burlington was back then, and I'm afraid at least some adults have not progressed much since then in their understanding. The conformity-oriented, white, straight Christian world in which I was raised was a primary impetus for my leaving the Midwest after graduating from college. But as a kid growing up, I was only aware that I felt out of place in my mostly homogenous world.

Despite all the advantages and comforts I enjoyed growing up white, upper middle class, smart, and athletic, I could not escape feeling different. I was never like others in my family, and few outside our family or the small circle of my parents' closest friends knew I was adopted. I was haunted by a vague but persistent feeling of loneliness.

Because of these feelings, I began to find comfort in solitude, like an old friend that had been lost to me. I sought solitude in my bedroom and in our large yard with its many pines, oaks, and maples. I would commune with nature on solo bike journeys to nearby fields and hidden gullies by the railroad tracks, and just wander around or sit for an hour—a good alternative to mowing the lawn and trimming the hedges. There I would daydream, concocting fantasies of the Old West, with me on my horse (my Schwinn bike) as a heroic cowboy on the lookout for "Indians" and bad guys. I saw myself as a star running back for the Iowa Hawkeyes or a home run-hitting teammate of Stan "the Man" Musial of the Saint Louis Cardinals.

In my teens, my fantasies extended to girls and young women. I imagined I was Bond—James Bond—accompanied by *Goldfinger's* Pussy Galore character or Jennifer Scott, the buxom blond who sat behind me in many high school classes. We often sat in alphabetical order, and every time I turned around to pass a paper to her, Jen's golden, shoulder-length blond hair hung teasingly before me. As I grew older, my fantasies shifted to literature, drinks with Ernest Hemingway and his pals at the Les Deux Magots in Paris, or dancing cheek-to-cheek with Daisy Buchanan at Jay Gatsby's mansion on West Egg.

However fulfilling these imaginal worlds were, loneliness continued to stalk me. No one in my family or circle of friends did anything to make me feel this way. I was never made to feel different, or unworthy of love. It's just that *something* was missing from my life; and in time I became more distant from my peers and even from my family.

When I got to high school, that nebulous feeling had gone underground, and I blossomed into the All-American Boy—adept with schoolwork, sports, and girls. I was elected junior class president and named one of the "Outstanding Seniors" in the high school yearbook. I had my own car—a used '64 Chevy Corvair with a stick shift. I was on my way to a good university. From the outside looking in, I had it made. *What could be the problem?*

6. Like a Bad Dream

When I was thirteen, I was standing in the kitchen with my mother. Behind her, were the double-door cabinets that contained shelves of pharmaceutical samples my dad had been given by drug company salesmen at his office. It was as well-stocked as a small commercial pharmacy, containing all manner of drugs to treat ailments ranging from anxiety, hemorrhoids, and ulcers to gout, heart palpitations, burns, high blood pressure, migraines, depression, and pain. I suspected my mother was fond of sampling what he brought home. She would act strange at times, with bursts of anger followed by periods of depression.

The cabinets also contained a full complement of first aid supplies stashed in a brown canvas satchel, which was tucked away on a top shelf and shielded from view my dad's holstered Smith & Wesson 38 Special. My parents were wary that someone might want to break into our house for these drugs. "You never know," Mom told me. "You have to be ready for anything. Some people might just kill you to get at your drugs. Ex-cons and drug addicts will do that. The same is true for some of those people from the South End."

I had been thinking more about my adoption and decided to take a chance and tell her that I wanted to know more. "Where did I come from? Will I ever know? What can you tell me?"

Suddenly my mom was growling like a cornered tomcat. Blue fire shot from her eyes and scorched my face with the power of a lightning-fast punch. She flew into a rage, her face flashing crimson, her bloodshot eyes popping out of their sockets. "What's wrong with you?" she hissed. "What do you think you need to know? Don't your father and I love you enough? What kind of gratitude is this? You've got a lot of nerve!"

I'm not sure I remember it all verbatim, but her exact words are not the point. Her self-righteous indignation caught me completely off guard, and her mission was accomplished. I shut up. I had no rejoinder and nothing to say in defense of my questions or my curiosity. I flushed with embarrassment and muttered something foul under my breath, as I scurried up the stairs two steps at a time to my room, where I slammed the door.

I'd never experienced such a furious onslaught of shame and humiliation. Now it was my turn for rage. I was blind to what was happening deep within me, but my mother's anger struck like a hot poker in the open wound of my soul. It hurt, and for a long time. I can still feel it today. I felt simultaneously exposed and invisible in that moment. I was stripped down—a feeling I would not allow myself to feel again for many years. As a consequence, I never spoke to her about my adoption, or about my years looking for answers, or my fateful reunion with my birth mother. Maybe I held back in spite. I don't say this with pride. It's a sad admission of holding on to my resentment much longer than was justified. Yet, I could not let go of it. Years later, before her death, I reconciled with Mom, but without words. It was an unforeseen moment of redemption for us both.

From this moment of shame and humiliation at age thirteen, I became determined to discover my identity and set course on my own path, separate from my family and hometown. I did so, not as a repudiation of my parent's love for me, nor mine for them. I heard a call, a voice beckoning me to my future self. I had no choice but to accept my fate, however uncharted the road ahead would be. This newly born quest was as precious to me as life itself.

PART TWO

Let the hard things break you. Let them affect you.
Let them change you.
Let these hard moments inform you.
Let this pain be your teacher.
The experiences of your life are trying to tell you something
about yourself.[2]
~ Pema Chödrön, Buddhist teacher and author ~

7. The President Has Been Shot

My future looked bright as I headed into junior high school.
School was going well. My athletic ability soared and I certainly
didn't lack for friends. But my world was disrupted like a news
bulletin interrupting a TV show. Like many Americans, national
events at the time shook me to the core.

In those days, all school-aged children participated in
duck-and-cover drills. We would ball up under our desks and
cover our heads and faces, preparing for a nuclear attack by the
Russians. Over time, we took these drills less seriously as we
realized that there is no real protection from an A-Bomb or an
H-Bomb. The destructive power of either would vastly eclipse the
bombs that leveled Hiroshima and Nagasaki in 1945. Burlington
was located halfway between Chicago and the Strategic Air
Command (SAC) near Omaha, Nebraska—both priority targets.
I couldn't get the image of blinding light out my mind; scorching
its way across Iowa, incinerating everything its path, killing us or
leaving us in agony to die.

My fear of the bomb was not abstract. As a young naval officer who served in the Pacific, my father brought back two mementos from Hiroshima: a small porcelain doll and a black leather Japanese Bible, both charred like half-toasted marshmallows. He was there just weeks after the devastation that killed a mostly civilian population of 350,000. The doll and the Bible sat on our living room shelf for years with no explanation how they came into his possession or why he kept them. I still wonder if the radiation in the dusty rubble of Hiroshima contributed to his death thirty years later, at the age of sixty-two, from a prolonged struggle with ALS.

I learned about the Cuban Missile Crisis in October 1962 from the *CBS Evening News* and the *Des Moines Register*. My parents never said a word about it, nor did the teachers at school, even though we were on the brink of a nuclear war. I knew it was too late to build a bomb shelter, but I did notice Mom quietly stockpiling canned goods and jugs of water in the root cellar in our basement. There was not much else to do but worry and wait.

The specter of nuclear extermination lurked in the back of my mind, where I sometimes saw myself being vaporized in a mushroom cloud. But, like the adults around me, I focused on my next biggest worries, which for me were winning football games and memorizing my lines for the school operetta.

All of it paled by comparison to the shock and grief that swept the nation when John F. Kennedy was assassinated on November 22, 1963. No one alive at the time can forget where and when they heard the news. It changed our lives and altered the course of history. It was a cloudy Friday afternoon and I was in Mr. McCurdy's ninth grade biology class at Oak Street Junior High. We were cleaning up our lab tables after dissecting frogs—a rather disgusting assignment. The principal's voice came over the PA system, his tone ominously unemotional.

"Your attention: teachers, boys, and girls. This is Mr. Keehn. I have an important announcement. The President has been shot in Dallas, Texas. He is now in emergency surgery. No details are available at this time. You will stay in your classrooms for the remainder of the day. No further school work is necessary, so please find a quiet activity. There will be no sports, music, or clubs after school. We have tried to notify your parents but you will not be dismissed early today. When school ends, please go home. That is all."

We sat in stunned silence. Some of the girls sniffled and blew their noses. I felt dizzy, so I asked to be excused to go the boys' restroom to wash my face and cool off. I was surprised to find I was the only one there. I took a deep breath and let out a big sob, which echoed off the tile walls and floor. When I heard other boys coming down the hallway, I wiped my eyes and stepped up to the urinal like nothing had happened. One guy tried to crack a stupid joke but I could see sadness on the faces of the other boys, so we quickly filed back to our classrooms without a word.

I watched TV the next day from morning until supper time, with endless reruns of the motorcade at Dealey Plaza, interviews with bystanders near the grassy knoll, statements by attending doctors and nurses at Parkland Hospital, and photos and names of those who conducted the autopsy. Then came news of another killing, a Dallas cop who had cornered the suspect of a different crime in a cheap movie theater. The name and picture of the suspected assassin were all over TV, along with many questions. A Russian or a CIA guy? Lee Harvey Oswald was arrested the same day, his high-powered rifle with a scope paraded in front of the press. *Got our man!* Rumors of a lynching, a cover-up, a Cuban or maybe a Russian conspiracy. Was the mob in on this? The assassination was in Texas, was Johnson in on it? But Texas Governor John Connelly got shot too. I didn't know what to think. And then there was Jackie Kennedy, standing alone for all the world to see, in her blood-stained pink suit and matching pillbox hat. She was such a sad sight to behold. I wondered what it would be like to return to the White House late at night with her children still asleep?

Our family did not go to church on November 24, but National Football League games played on like it was any other Sunday. I stayed glued to the TV, the steady drone of the news becoming tedious. Suddenly, CBS news broke to live coverage in the basement of the Dallas police station where Lee Harvey Oswald was being transferred in handcuffs to the county jail. I heard a faint pop and saw a scrum of men in police uniforms, dark suits, and cowboy hats. Someone yelled, "He's been hit!" I saw for a moment Oswald's slight body lying on the ground, clutching his gut in agony. Then the cops grabbed a guy in a heavy overcoat and hat. I saw a pistol, and someone was saying they had the man that killed Oswald: Jack Ruby, Dallas night club owner with possible mob connections. It was total pandemonium—an actual murder on live television! I was already on so much overload, I didn't know what to do or say. I stayed riveted to the television for weeks.

Then came Monday and the President's state funeral procession and burial. I was crouched in front of the TV long enough to see John-John salute his father's coffin as it rolled by. The day was sunny, but windy and cold, and the horses of the caisson were jittery. The riderless horse, with cavalry boots strapped backward in the stirrups of the saddle, was especially nervous. Something wasn't right. I slipped away from my parents and the TV room and retreated upstairs to my bedroom, where I swung my brown stuffed chair toward the window to face the leafless red maple tree outside. I turned on my portable transistor radio and hunkered down. I heard the somber prayers and final remarks by dignitaries at the Arlington National Cemetery gravesite. The voices of the newscasters hushed to a whisper. Then it happened. Knowing I was alone and safe in my room where no one could hear me, I burst into tears. They streamed down my cheeks and soaked into my sweater. I grabbed a pillow from my bed and held it tight across my face to mute the sound. I felt I was falling into a deep abyss. I stayed in my room all afternoon, and came down to supper only after I was called.

The crises and tragedies of early 1960s felt like major turning points. They changed the course of my life in directions not then known, and I'm sure that was true for many others as well. The confusion and mystery of the President's death hung a like a dark shadow over the nation for months. Grief was in the air. The President's death was real and terribly sad. But these events also opened something in me that felt deep and necessary.

8. It's the Sixties!

My spirits lifted in early 1964. The Beatles burst onto the scene, making their incredible American debut on the *Ed Sullivan Show* on February 9, 1964—a day before my fifteenth birthday. Two weeks later, twenty-two-year-old Cassius Clay, soon to become Muhammad Ali, beat up the hulking thug Sonny Liston for the Heavyweight Boxing Championship. Malcolm X broke with Elijah Muhammad and the Nation of Islam a few weeks after that. In August, a ginned-up report of an attack on the *USS Maddox* in the Gulf of Tonkin off the coast of North Vietnam provided President Johnson and Congress the bogus excuse to ramp up the war in Vietnam. Nelson Mandela was sentenced to life imprisonment that year for defying South African policies of Apartheid. The Free Speech Movement picked up speed and made Mario Savio a cult hero of the Left. Republican presidential candidate Barry Goldwater declared, "Extremism in defense of liberty is no vice!" Goldwater would fit right in today with the Proud Boys. The Civil Rights Act was signed by President Johnson. The Ford Mustang was produced. Clint Eastwood made the first of his many Spaghetti Westerns. Sidney Poitier was the first Black man to win Best Actor for his role in *Lilies of the Field*.

These popular songs rose to the top of the charts: "Pretty Woman" (Roy Orbison), "Chapel of Love" (The Dixie Cups), "The Little Old Lady from Pasadena" (Jan and Dean), and my all-time favorite, "House of the Rising Sun" (The Animals). The Sixties were a great time to be a teenager. Most of us weren't on drugs, at least not yet, but we were flying high, as my tenth-grade class entered Burlington High School in the fall of 1964.

High school began well enough. It was easy and fun. I had plenty of girlfriends and buddies. I excelled in history, English, and Latin. I did what I had to do to pull good grades in math and chemistry. I had a terrible crush on my French teacher, Mademoiselle Moreau, who had just graduated from college earlier that spring. I burst with furtive pride from the rumor that she and I were having an affair. It was true that she lived down the street from me in a small bungalow; and I had, in fact, visited her with a friend on one occasion. But an affair? I only wished!

Contrary to my reputation, I was rather shy with girls when I got closer to them. There was no way I could handle a clandestine relationship with a teacher, though only four years older than me. That said, I seemed to have a new girlfriend every few months. I wasn't unhappy with any of them, but I was searching for something I couldn't find in another person. That pattern continued for years.

But something else began to flourish in me, too. I began to read the pioneers of psychology like Sigmund Freud and C. G. Jung. I fell in love with *Summerhill: A Radical Approach to Childrearing* by radical British educator A.S. Neill. And I became familiar with theologians like Harvey Cox and Paul Tillich. I was so enthralled by theology, I thought I might attend the Union Theological Seminary in New York after graduating. I vaguely recall getting these books from a somewhat shady bookstore downtown that sold mostly magazines and cigarettes. My books were completely out of step with my family, school and peers. The topics were hard for me to grasp, as I lacked the necessary context and intellectual rigor. Nevertheless, I plowed my way through some and skimmed others. The seeds of these early interests would grow and blossom years later. I also joined the Columbia Record Club and purchased LPs of all kinds. I built a small but eclectic collection that included Thelonious Monk, Hank Williams, Stan Getz, and Ray Charles. It was a simple and secret pleasure to be unique and independent in the eyes of no one but me.

Another thing that set me apart from others, or so I thought, was my capacity for dreaming. I had a vivid imagination when I played alone, and my daytime imagination would slip into my sleep at night. My dreams as a young child had been of adventures, featuring TV heroes like Superman and the Lone Ranger. Not until my teen years did I gingerly inquire of friends whether they too saw mini-movies in their heads during their sleep. Some would shake their heads, like I was half-insane. Others confused my use of the term *dream*, with an aspiration, like *I dreamed I would someday play in the backfield with Gale Sayers and the Chicago Bears*. So, I kept my mouth shut and closed off the mystery of my dream world from others. I wished I could have a conversation about dreams with someone who could help me understand what I was experiencing. So, I turned to Freud's *The Interpretation of Dreams*. He said that dreams were the expression of our deepest desires and that they represented the "royal road" to the unconscious. I could barely grasp these concepts and knew no one I could talk to about them, yet they stayed with me and surfaced later in my life.

Six years later, I wrote one of my college theses on dreams and dreaming, combining the new science of sleep with insights from Freud and Jung. And forty-five years after that, I immersed myself in depth psychology, which led me to become a psychotherapist.

These newly acquired interests did not, thankfully, set me apart from my friends. My social life was always in high gear. I was one of the best guys to party with; and I loved team sports, and was a good teammate. But life at home was different. My intellectual interests, athletic ability, and political preferences were at odds with everyone else in my family. As my siblings grew older, it was evident that they resembled each other and not me. By the time I was fifteen, as the rest of the family geared up for summer camping trips, I wanted to stay home, work a summer job, get in shape for the football season, and hang out with friends. These differences were a constant reminder that their genetic code was not like mine. Their tastes and interests were nearly identical, and mine were not like theirs.

These glaring differences made me want to know more about my blood relatives, specifically the woman who gave birth to me—my *other* mother. Who was she? Was she alive? Where did she live? Why did she give me up in the first place? Perhaps it was these questions, or their answers, that made me feel so alone.

In those pre-internet days, without the physical or technical ability to search for adoption agencies in Iowa or Missouri, I had no way of finding answers on my own. My parents were no help, as I refused to bring up the issue of my adoption. I could only bide my time until I was in college with my own mailing address. Then I began writing letters of inquiry about my birth and adoption, clueless about how difficult that would be. It was another twenty years before a twist of fate placed a few important pieces of the puzzle in my hands. What I did know, even in high school, was that the flame of curiosity was burning in me. I was determined to find my birth mother by any means necessary, whether she was dead or alive. Of course, I dearly hoped to find her alive.

9. Mr. G and Me

With so much going on in high school, I had little time to stew about my adoption. As a junior, I was starting on the varsity football team. Our team was ranked number one in the state by mid-October. Between schoolwork and football practice, there was time for little else except Saturday night dates and parties. Then, out of the blue, I received an invitation that would change my life.

A smart, popular senior named Pamela approached me after school. Although she lived in our neighborhood, I didn't know her well. She beckoned me out of hearing range of other students and spoke in a hushed tone. She was delivering a message from my former English teacher from junior high.

"I'm a big fan of Mr. Galloway, and I believe you are too. He told me he wants you to come over to his house on Saturday afternoon. Can you? Gerard Hanson [another brainy senior] and I have been meeting with him for about a year to talk about books, and he reads what we write. I think that's why he wants to see you. Don't tell anyone at school. It's kind of a private thing."

The prospect of being mentored by Mr. Galloway was beyond my wildest dreams. Bob Galloway, or Mr. G as we called him, was legendary in the eyes of his students. His looks were pretty standard for the day. He wore a short-sleeved dress shirt with a skinny clip-on black tie, as was the custom for male teachers. He had a bit of receding hairline and a little beer belly that hung over his belt. He carried a pack of Chesterfields in his front shirt pocket. In the heat of elaborating on the literary subject of the day, he would belly laugh and jump up and down, jettisoning cigarettes from his pocket onto the classroom floor. Some of the kids in the front row would try to crib a few, which he never said a word about.

I had worked hard in his class and got good grades. I was flattered that he liked my writing. I hung on his every word and gesture and thought about him all the time, like having a crush. He particularly appealed to those of us planning to go to college, but what I admired most about him was the way he treated the kids who were poor—the kids whose families held no expectations for them about school. I knew that after high school, some would enlist in the military and others would work on an assembly line at Case Tractor or Champion Spark Plug. He treated each of those kids with real respect.

It was common to see him put his arm around one of them as they left class for the day. "Hey kid!" he'd say. "Great to have you show up today! You know, you're a lot smarter than you think—don't forget that! Thanks for not tearing the place up today because the maid doesn't come until Friday! Do your homework tonight if you don't get arrested for loitering down by the Sombrero [a popular dive-bar downtown]!"

Then he would howl with laughter and so would they. They knew it was a joke, and they loved him for making them feel special. No other teacher treated them that way. People crudely referred to these kids as "white trash," and they knew it. Mr. Galloway knew more about them and their lives at home than they realized, and it turned out, the same was true for me. He knew things about me I didn't yet know about myself. But I knew he saw something special in me and that was all that mattered.

Years later, as a teacher and then as a psychotherapist, I worked with kids of all ages and backgrounds. At times, I could hear Mr. G's words spill from my mouth, as though I were channeling him. I developed a way with kids that I hope was as authentic and endearing as he had been. I learned from him how to find something unique and special about each person.

Mr. G had left Oak Street Junior High by the time I entered Burlington High School. He had clashed with Principal Elroy Petty over funds for teaching summer courses at the University of Iowa. Petty, a man well-named, had reneged on the agreement. Principal Petty was short with dark-rimmed glasses. His greasy crew cut looked out of date, as did the baggy suit he wore every day. He was a small man in every way. He enjoyed intimidating the weak, but he ingratiated himself to the parents, especially those of high social status.

Everyone knew that Elroy Petty resented Mr. Galloway for his reputation as the best teacher in the school. I suspect Petty baited Galloway into an argument, and whether out of spite or pride, Mr. G quit teaching completely just before the school year started. He was quickly hired as the county probation officer, which was a good fit for a man who got on well with juvenile delinquents. He had a soft spot for young people who had gotten into trouble. But my heart ached knowing I would not have him for a teacher when I started tenth grade in high school.

That first private meeting with Mr. G seems like yesterday. On a blustery Saturday afternoon in early October, he ushered me into his library. Pamela and Gerard were not there. I had Mr. G to myself for a whole afternoon! I felt as if I'd tumbled into his private kingdom, where I was the prince-in-training. Books were crammed to the ceiling on rickety wooden shelves lining three walls. I paced by rows of books, perusing their titles. Though unfamiliar with many of them, I knew they covered all manner of fiction and nonfiction. I stood back in awe, as if seeing fire for the first time.

In the course of many Saturday afternoons to come, Mr. G introduced me to the American canon of Hemingway, Fitzgerald, and Steinbeck. He later sent me home with works by existentialists such as Camus and Sartre. Most intriguing to me was his collection of poetry. Once he picked a poem by e. e. cummings, "[love is more thicker than forget]," and had me read it aloud. I would do the same with "The Red Wheelbarrow," by William Carlos Williams. I'd read the poem, then he would ask me to read it again, more slowly. He was teaching me to savor the sounds, the cadence, and the shape of words.

Something of this poetry reading ritual surely stayed with me. I wrote my second college thesis on William Carlos Williams and the imagist movement in modern poetry. There's no doubt that my early interest in Williams and imagism was prescient. Today, archetypal and dream images are central to my work in Jungian and archetypal psychology. But as a young high schooler,

I felt seen by Mr. G in a way I'd never experienced with family or friends. I knew from the beginning we were kindred spirits.

One crisp December Saturday afternoon, we took a break in in the alley behind his house. It was nearly time for me to go home. To my great surprise, he offered me a can of Hamm's beer and one of his Chesterfields. I accepted. "If your old man finds out about this," he said, "he'll have us both locked up in Fort Madison," by which he meant the site of the Iowa State Penitentiary. "You don't want that to happen. I'll be a lousy cellmate. I snore!"

We laughed, knowing that I would keep my mouth shut. We leaned on the hood of his powder-blue 1962 Plymouth Fury, letting dusk quietly settle around us. I took a deep drag off that cigarette and let it sink deeply into my lungs before blowing a long thin trail of smoke upward to the darkening sky.

"Hamm's—the beer refreshing!" we chanted, and then cackled like chickens in rain.

Mr. G insisted that I write. "I don't care what you write," he said. "Just make it your own and bring it back next time. Whatever you do, don't spill any beer on my books and let the cops take them away when you get pulled over for a DUI!" Then he would do that belly laugh of his. I knew I was getting the treatment.

I wrote quite a few poems that fall and winter, which I gave to him for his comments and approval. To my shock, Mr. G abruptly moved away in the spring. My tutorials ended just like that. He had a better paying parole officer job in Keokuk. He would also teach English at the maximum-security penitentiary in nearby Fort Madison. He later told me that a couple of his inmate-students in prison were young men he had taught in high school. This was no surprise to either of us.

We corresponded for a while, until after I left for college, when we lost track of each other. Forty years later, I Googled him and discovered that he was living with his second wife near Keosauqua, Iowa, an hour's drive from my hometown. On the day of our reunion, I pulled up to their red brick farmhouse in a rental car. As he sauntered to the sliding glass door to welcome me, I could see he had noticeable limp. He had aged but he was still Mr. G.

He greeted me as I knew he would: "Hey, kid! Great to see you." And without another word, he exclaimed, "I've got some of your poetry from high school. Want to see it?" He pulled a thick file folder from his oak cabinet and handed it to me with a twinkle in his eye. I shot a quick glance back his way, knowing what was coming next. He pulled a couple of beers from the fridge, gesturing toward the back porch. He sat quietly, diligently watching me leaf through pieces I had written half a century before. I didn't try to hide my tears. I didn't need to. Even that afternoon in the alley behind Mr. G's house, sharing the first beer and cigarette with him, could not top this moment.

10. How Dreams Die

Something else changed in my life that autumn. The Burlington High football team was still near the top of the state rankings. Playing on a state championship team was a dream come true. Earlier in the season, I'd been assigned to replace a senior lineman, who was out for the season with an injury. I fit in quickly, although I was crestfallen not to play running back. There's a lot of room for glory as a running back, not so much for a lineman. I preferred stardom. I had been dreaming of playing football since growing up near the Iowa Hawkeye Football Stadium. I had spent every summer since the sixth grade lifting weights and running intervals on the golf course before dark. I kept a record of my daily sit-ups and pushups and watched or listened to as much college and professional football as I could. I followed all the teams in the Big Ten and Pac-8, and made predictions in September for which teams would make it to the Rose Bowl on New Year's Day. Football was my life.

By the beginning of my junior year, I received inquiries from college football scouts and recruiters. These tended to be small colleges from Iowa and none of them appealed to me academically. I kept my opinions to myself, as most of my coaches had played at those schools. The biggest-name recruiter I talked with was from the Air Force Academy. As much as I liked Colorado, I was not going to play for a military school—not when the war in Viet Nam was heating up. I kept that opinion to myself, too. Beyond the flattery of recruitment, I remained in a minor state of ecstasy as our team continued to win. When things clicked and our team did well, we were like a family. I loved that. I felt like I belonged. I had earned the right to be a starter on the team, a very big deal to me.

The drudgery of practice was another story. It was ungodly tedious, especially in the sweltering humidity of late summer and freezing rain of early winter. The dull repetition of football practice was broken quickly as we prepared to play our league rival in the Quad Cities. It was a simple scene with an ending that never changed. Yet the memory of it stays with me like a recurring nightmare.

> A running play is over, a coach blows his whistle, and the play is dead. I am struggling to regain my footing as I arise from a pile of hulky linemen. You can't tell the difference between us, our muddied practice jerseys smeared with the same shade of brown. I sense a body coming toward me from the left at the edge of my peripheral vision, as if in slow motion. This can't be anything—the ball's dead, the play is long over. But this body is indeed flying toward me like a plummeting airplane about to crash. It's heading for my left leg, which is planted like a flagpole in a pile of anomalous bodies. There is a sound, blunt and

loud, like the snap of a broom handle. I begin
to topple onto the cleat-mauled field, but there's
nowhere to fall and I tilt awkwardly in mid-air.
I make no cry anyone can hear. My pain instead
becomes a blinding flash of color, searing through
the field of my vision, like volcanic fire erupting.

I was taken straight to the emergency room. Now, when
I needed my dad the most, he was out of town at a conference.
Another surgeon examined me and put me in traction for the night
at Burlington Hospital. The prognosis was not good. I would need
surgery as soon as possible. My mother drove me to University of
Iowa Hospital the next day where I was admitted to the orthopedic
wing, less than a mile from where we once lived.

Dad arrived from Chicago the following day just in time to
watch the surgery, which was conducted by his former colleague,
Rudy Carlson, Chief of Orthopedics. As I woke up in the recovery
room, Dr. Carlson glibly assured me the cartilage removal was a
success. I'd be in a cast for a few weeks, he said. He was confident
that after physical therapy, I might be able to play part of the
basketball season, and for sure, I'd be ready for track season in the
spring. I was young and strong, and I was going to be fine. They
had taken out a chunk of torn meniscus from one side of the knee
joint, which at the time was considered state-of-the-art surgery.

That promise sounded great, but turned out to be one big
fat lie, which I suspected at the time. Hovering over my body in the
recovery room, and before I appeared to be conscious, Dr. Carlson
spoke directly to my dad in a hushed tone from behind his surgical
mask, "Well, Bob, I'm still concerned that the joint doesn't want to
straighten itself out. If it doesn't, we can knock him out again and
just bend it into place. He might need another surgery."

I wanted to fade away into my anesthetic haze, but the
acrid the scent of ammonia brought me to full attention. I tilted
my head upward from the pillow of the sheeted gurney and looked

down my torso toward my knee. What I saw was a large white cast hanging from a pulley, my leg torqued at an unnatural angle in the air. This was disconcerting to say the least. Now I knew for sure something was not right. I didn't look right and it sure as hell didn't feel right. Two casts and six months later, my worst fear was realized. My leg was permanently damaged, never able to fully straighten or bend. My hopes of playing football again at a competitive level were crushed dead.

I stayed in the University Hospital for six nights. My mother had a family to tend to, and my dad had to get back to his own patients, so I was relegated to a private room in the ortho wing. I had a remote-control TV in the corner of the ceiling and the nurses brought me magazines from the ward's waiting room—ones that appealed to farmers and soap opera fans. That was it for entertainment. But I was so doped up, doing nothing seemed like the best and only thing to do.

Mom made one midweek trip to see me. She was not bringing my copy of Steinbeck's *Of Mice and Men* to read—not with that racy jacket cover that she complained about—the one with a floozy country girl with a low-cut blouse who looked like sexy movie star Jane Russell. I was living an existential horror show, so I was not in the mood for Camus. I amused myself thinking Mom might bring my copy of *I and Thou* and maybe she would confuse Martin Buber's author photo with Gabby Hayes, as both had bushy gray beards. I imagined she would think it was a biography about Gabby's days playing sidekick to Hopalong Cassidy. Pain killers and all, I laughed out loud at the thought. I wasn't completely dead. I could still amuse myself.

To Mom's credit, she brought my girlfriend Janelle with her to Iowa City, which was nice but a little weird. I wondered what they talked about in the car? I hoped Janelle would play dumb while answering questions related to our dating, such as, *where do we go and what do we do?* But then fortune smiled upon us. I got a few minutes alone with Janelle—time for a quick kiss while

Mom went for coffee. Despite the side effects of the sedatives and my mind-numbing constipation, when Janelle bent over the bed rail to kiss me goodbye, she slid my hand under her blouse, which triggered a jolt of titillating energy beneath my hospital gown. I knew all was not lost. This was another sign of life in me.

I did not take hospitalization well, though. I was seriously self-pitying—the All-American boy brought low. Woe is me. Despite the cheery pep talks I got from the nurses, I felt wrapped in a straitjacket of depression. When the doctors and staff left me to the emptiness of my hospital room each evening, I sometimes teared up, as I had in the aftermath of the President's assassination. Like the deep and complicated emotions attached to my grief over Kennedy, the tears over my broken knee and shattered dreams were real enough.

I am sure the cocktail of painkillers, self-pity, and loneliness contributed to my gloom; but even then, I suspected there was something else, as my sadness continued to pull me under. With so much time and so little to do, I began to retrace my life all the way back to the beginning—whatever or wherever that was. All the questions I held about my adoption soon drifted back, haunting me like Jacob Marley's ghost. Feeling small and alone in my hospital bed, with my leg hitched up in the air, there was little else to do but stare out the window at the Hawkeye Football Stadium mocking me in the distance. I wondered what was going to become of me? If football was not going to be part of my future, what was?

Dr. Carlson's secret prediction came true. I returned to Iowa City for another surgery and lived for four more months with crutches and a half-cast. After all that torture, my knee remained swollen with a limited range of motion. I managed to play football in the fall, but I was not back in true form. I might have fooled others, but I was not kidding myself. I couldn't run like I used to. To make matters worse, our team won only one game that season.

The losses were humiliating, but our losing season and my ruined knee proved to be a good lesson in failure.

By November, the season was over, my leg was over, and football was over for me forever. These were crystal-clear facts, but I had a hard time accepting them. In the long run, it was a benefit to know what hitting a wall actually felt like—in body and soul. This would prepare me for another time, worse than this. But the sense of who I was in the world rudely faded away. The two things I wanted the most were lost to me: my other mother and my image as a football hero. Who was I now? All I really knew was that my crushing losses meant little to anyone else. Something inside me knew I had to rebound and get over myself. It was time to grow up and find a new way to be in the world.

11. Summer of Shock, Summer of Love

The Summer of Love sprang to life in San Francisco in 1967, but not in my hometown. I was isolated. I knew little of what was really happening in Haight-Ashbury or anywhere on the West Coast except for the music I listened to and the sardonic accounts I read in *U.S. News & World Report*. Something was in the air but I felt left behind. In the words of fellow Burlingtonian and New York Literary agent, Sterling Lord, whose parents lived two houses from mine:

> The free-swinging and energetic world of Jack Kerouac and Allen Ginsberg and the atmosphere of the Beat Generation were light years apart from the pleasant, orderly Iowa town where I grew up. In some ways, Burlington, Iowa represented the life the Beats were trampling on in the fifties and sixties.[3]

My graduating class was the last straight class at Burlington High School. No one had smoked pot or dropped acid. Tie-dyed T-shirts and bell-bottom jeans were just becoming popular. Long hair for boys back then meant your hair was touching your ears. Mini-skirts for girls hung just above the knee. Although some of us opposed the war in Viet Nam, none of us had ever been in a demonstration. Major cultural events and social upheaval were things we understood only from TV and movies. The social and political transformation of our generation was taking place elsewhere. The cultural shifts of the Sixties were not impacting our daily lives, at least not yet.

That summer I served as an orderly in the Psychiatric Unit of Burlington Hospital. I reported each morning to the head nurse for staff meetings, which were, more accurately, gossip sessions about patients. They avoided talking about hospital doctors around me, although Dad was popular and respected by everyone. They liked a doctor who didn't condescend to nurses or patients.

I was responsible for helping patients finish their breakfasts and then I'd organize an activity for the morning, such as making ceramic ashtrays. I'd sometimes accompany a nurse to a patient's room if he or she was being uncooperative, which wasn't often, as most were blitzed by their morning cocktail of pills. Thorazine was the drug of choice for our town's only psychiatrist, Dr. Enoch Morison. My mother whispered in my direction that he was a quack and an alcoholic. Morison's idea of doing rounds was talking with the head nurse and conducting therapy sessions with patients that lasted only a few minutes. I had hoped that as a favor to my dad, he would pull me aside every now and then, and explain what he was doing. It didn't happen. His presence on the unit was sporadic, and even when he was there, wearing his tweed sports jacket and dress slacks, he looked disheveled and tired with bloodshot eyes.

One morning, I was asked to help restrain a patient who was undergoing electroshock treatment. A veteran nurse's assistant,

47

Miss O'Brien, led me to small room and began to explain the procedure, when an eighty-year-old woman was wheeled in. We then helped transfer her to the surgery table. When Dr. Morison entered the room, he looked at Miss O'Brien and me and stated coldly, "When she goes into convulsions, just hold her down." That was all.

I wasn't altogether surprised to smell alcohol on his breath at 9:15 a.m. His hands were shaking as tried to insert a syringe into the woman's forearm vein to administer a sedative. He missed the first two times and then succeeded the third time with the assistance of the head nurse's steady hand. The room was tense.

The head nurse applied K-Y Jelly to the patient's temples, then tightly clamped small steel electrode plates over them and inserted a large, rubber stopper into her mouth, like a boxer's mouth piece. Dr. Morison then cranked up the dial on the machine that was to administer the blast which was supposed to bring an elderly lady's brains back into reality.

When Dr. Morison hit the switch, the patient's body twitched so hard, her head flipped off the pillow. Then she fell back, flat and limp, and she didn't move, not a hair. We all stood there as she turned blue, then gray, then a shade of dirty dishwater. Clearly, she wasn't breathing. I gathered from the looks of the nursing staff that something was wrong.

"Doctor, I don't think she's breathing. Do you think we should give her artificial respiration?" No response from Dr. Morison. "Doctor? Doctor? What should we do now?"

Finally, he took out his stethoscope to confirm the obvious. He then began to pound her tiny chest with his clumpy fist. He told us to turn her over so he could do artificial respiration the old-fashioned way. Eventually, we heard her cough, so we rolled her over. Two or three minutes passed before she started to convulse in tiny spasmatic waves. Still deathly pale, she began to breathe a little and make small whimpering sounds. Dr. Morison then removed his stethoscope from around his neck and glanced briefly at the head nurse, his white shirt saturated with sweat.

In a sheepish tone, he muttered, "I guess she'll be fine. Give me a call this afternoon if you need to. Otherwise, I'll be back tomorrow."

And that was it. He turned on his heels and left the room. I had never been to medical school, so what did I know? But I was pretty sure I had just seen a doctor nearly kill a patient who had no business being electroshocked in the first place. This was my initiation to the world of psychiatry and modern therapeutic treatment for major mental disorders, or so I was led to believe.

Luckily for me, the Summer of Love was about falling in love. Janelle and I started seeing each other again after a hiatus. With fewer parties to go to, we found more time to be alone. We were increasingly intimate—physically and emotionally. Her parents were gone from home a lot, so our frequent rendezvous brought us closer to the inevitable. We were open, exploratory, and decidedly mutual in our desire to please each other. When we weren't panting and frolicking, we talked endlessly and watched what movies we could find on television. It was a great time for us, even though we knew we would soon be heading in different directions.

I loved who she was: bright, animated, and charismatic. She looked a little like movie star Melissa McCarthy—very cute, a little plump, and with a wicked sense of humor. Yet there was also an innocence to her that was genuine. I admired her ease simply being herself.

The tale of consummating our love at the end of the summer was actually quite sweet. I will offer no further details, but it was a nice send-off to college. By today's standards, not having sex before age eighteen would seem old-fashioned. As you have learned, I was big into girls and I went out with more than my fair share. I can see now how much I wanted to be liked and loved, and by more than one girl. You may correctly guess that I was in search of something that felt out of reach. I could not stay with one girl for very long. It was different with Janelle. Our romance was driven in part by the predictable desires of our bodies, but it went beyond that. We had what the French call *affaire de coeur*, an affair of the heart. With Janelle, I realized that I could not experience genuine pleasure without a deep friendship and the security and confidences that come with that. Without survey results in hand, I suspect this is not the case for many men.

My desire for intimacy woven around friendship may sound unusual for an eighteen-year-old. Admittedly, I may have had this particular kind of desire wired into me, whether I was adopted or not. But I was adopted. I had no known family tree to help me trace back the threads of my tastes, vices, and penchants concerning love and relationships. A high school love affair was just that. My relationship with Janelle was a milestone that fused something deeper into me. I was ready to break from the role in which I'd been cast in high school. After our time together, I was ready to forge my own path.

Leaving for the University of Wisconsin was a high priority. I was eager to break away from my home and my high school world. Once away, I thought, I'd be free to investigate the mystery of my adoption and my birth parents. But I could not foresee the events that were about to transform me—and thousands of other fresh-faced undergraduates in Madison. Fate had its way with me and my generation. Events shook me awake, and there was no going back. I became a student radical overnight.

PART THREE

But we are not our history; ultimately, we are what
wishes to enter the world through us, though to
underestimate the power of that history
as an invisible player in the choices of daily life is a grave error.[4]
~ James Hollis, Jungian analyst and writer ~

12. Drawing the Line

I arrived at the University of Wisconsin in August 1967 full of excitement. The sprawling Madison campus was pristine. My limestone brick dormitory that overlooked a white-capped Lake Mendota was quintessential as well. The Student Union, which also sat next to Lake Mendota, was just a mile away. The Union was an enticing place where eighteen-year-olds could legally drink beer in its cavernous Rathskeller—the hub of campus activity. Camp Randall, the Badger football stadium, was nearby, as was Babcock Hall, home of the famous dairy and ice-cream store. My new dormmates hailed from New York, Chicago, and many cities and small towns across Wisconsin. I was the only student in my dorm from Iowa and it probably showed. I was as wide-eyed as if I had crashed-landed in the Land of Oz.

I was humbled and excited by so many things I had never experienced: bagels with cream cheese, tacos, heated arguments between Zionist and Palestinian students, green beer on Saint Patrick's Day on State Street, bratwurst sandwiches, rabid Green Bay Packers fans, and the nasally Wisconsin dialect that pronounced its state name Wizz-káhn-sen, and Milwaukee with a missing syllable: Mmwóckie.

I participated in Rush Week sponsored by the fraternities that lined Langdon Street, and joined Sigma Chi, the largest. I was chosen as president of the pledge class. I had no clue why, as I barely knew any of my fellow pledges. Other than organizing a get-together with the pledge class girls of the Tri-Delt sorority, I remember very little of being a Sigma Chi, as I stayed with it for only two months. When I got around to reading the fine print of the Sigma Chi Charter, I discovered a *whites-only* clause. In those days, *whites-only* also meant no Jews. I left for good, even before the drunken excesses of initiation.

When I went home at Thanksgiving, I deposited the remnants of what I had thought I would need to become a real college man—my three-piece herringbone suit and wing-tip shoes, never to be worn again. By then, my daily attire had become bell-bottom jeans and blue work shirts—the *in* look at the time. My new wardrobe announced to the world that I had abandoned my bourgeois background in exchange for something more proletarian, or more like Jerry Garcia and Bob Dylan. My parents did not openly object my new looks. But Mom kept giving me the evil eye, asking silently, "What's up with this boy? Is he on drugs?" I thought the answers were quite evident.

But my world had changed long before Thanksgiving. On an otherwise gorgeous afternoon in mid-October, a peaceful campus protest at the Commerce Building took an unexpected and violent turn. Without warning, a phalanx of Dane County sheriff's deputies and University police attacked two hundred students who were sitting tightly bunched in the front hallway of the Commerce Building. Their protest was directed at the on-campus presence of Dow Chemical, the manufacturer of napalm, a volatile petrochemical being used by the US in Vietnam—burning forests, combatants, and civilians. Without provocation, the police waded into the protesters with billy clubs flailing. You could hear the students' screams from blocks away. Many were badly beaten in the vicious onslaught. We later learned that this police action was an insurrection, likely planned by the cops in advance to teach the hippies and "communists" a lesson.

Five thousand students and many young faculty members pressed toward the mêlée and were met with a barrage of teargas cannisters launched in every direction by the police, who had already put on their gas masks. The teargas formed a dense cloud, and people gagged, panicked, and scattered. It was a horrific spectacle to behold, as I well know. I was one of those students. Whatever innocence I'd brought to the University of Wisconsin vaporized, as thousands of students like me were radicalized in an instant. Just like that, the lines were clearly drawn between us and them.

Everything changed. There'd be no more naïve demonstrations and no more asking for parade permits. We were united against more than just the war in Viet Nam. We opposed the Chancellor, the University, the Dane County Sheriff, Chief of the Campus Police, the Madison Police Department, the Governor, and the Wisconsin State Legislature—*the system.* As it turned out, the University remained at war with its own faculty and students during my entire college experience.

Two days after the debacle at the Commerce Building, I was on my way to an Honors English class on Bascom Hill taught by Stuart Curran, a popular professor known for his spellbinding lectures on Romantic poets and for his androgenous good looks. Both men and women loved him. The class was small, and I came prepared. But as I approached the building, a dozen students had formed a picket line by the front entrance. The organizers had made demands of the Chancellor and vowed to close the campus if these demands weren't met. The protestors pleaded for us to join them. A line had been drawn, and if you crossed it, you'd be on the side with the administration and therefore on the side of war. If you didn't, you'd be aligned with thousands of students who vehemently opposed the university's politics and the war. It felt more like a moral choice than a political one.

I was torn. I desperately wanted to attend this provocative class and get on with my interests in literature and writing. But as I noticed a few students slink across the line and sheepishly scamper into the building through a side door, I knew I couldn't. To hell with the administration, I thought, and to hell with the student organizers. I had to make this decision for myself, not for them. So, I joined the picket line and went on strike. I felt like I knew who I was for the first time in my life and I liked it.

13. Puzzle Pieces

Although my focus was on schoolwork and campus politics, the unknowns about my adoption nagged at me throughout college. In early 1970, at the beginning of the second semester of my junior year, I initiated the first of a series of letters to C.W. O'Rourke, director of the American Home Finding Association in Ottumwa. I still have much of this correspondence, and the dissonance between his genuine responsiveness and his paternalistic tone is startling. In his first response, he reminded me that my official records were sealed and could not be opened except by court order. My claim that "I have a right to know" did not cut it with him. He suggested I write him again and with specific questions to which he could give specific answers. I did so immediately and his response took my breath away. The information he shared was the first of many pieces I needed to complete the puzzle. Highlights of his two-page, single spaced letter included:

- My birth mother was a high school graduate and had achieved supervisory status as a nurse. She liked to sing, played several instruments, and had a keen interest in world affairs and political science. She belonged to the Presbyterian Church.

- She was attractive, with black hair and brown eyes. She had "regular features, in good proportion." She had an outgoing personality. Her father labeled her as an extrovert.
- My birth father was a college graduate with a major in business. He excelled in sports at college. He was "a very pleasant person, both in appearance and personality. He was popular with his friends." His interests included music and reading.
- Both birth parents were in good health and had no history of hereditary disease.

O'Rourke invited me to contact him again if I had more questions, which I did. I didn't save a copy of my letter but I believe I thanked him for what he sent me. My inquiry prompted another timely reply. He told me that my birth parents were not married to each other, as it was "impossible and impractical for them to be married since your father was already married." Well, now. He continued, stating that my birth mother wanted me to be in a home with both a mother and a father.

"It is not a matter whether she didn't want you, but rather where she put her own desires aside and took the course of action which she believed would best safeguard your future." Hmm.

This letter did not end with another offer to correspond with him. I interpreted his response as a pat on the head and a message not to bother him again: "Stephen, there is nothing to be gained in delving further into the past. Your academic record would indicate that you are an achiever. Therefore, I would suggest that your focus on the future, considering, as they say, 'Today is the first day of the rest of your life.'"

So, there it was. I was an illegitimate child, fathered by a guy who was already married. At least I knew this much. But O'Rourke's condescending tone and sloganeering send-off made me furious. His tone rankles me to this day. Like my mother's rebuke, O'Rourke's admonishment only stoked the fire of my curiosity and drive.

I sent one more letter to O'Rourke in 1972, and again, his response was immediate.

> In the last year we have had several requests for "birth time" and realize that it is important from an *astrological* [emphasis mine] aspect. However, that is one detail that seems to be missing from our past records....I am sorry to disappoint you.

I was surprised that he used the word *astrology*, as I did not refer to it in my letter to him. His reply to me is ironic today, as I later trained at the Centre for Psychological Astrology in London. It was then that I came to understand the importance of a birth time in a natal chart—what certain schools of astrology consider to be the roadmap of our life's destiny. I could have used such a roadmap at the time. I was lost—and to make matters worse, I didn't know it. This letter was the last I heard from O'Rourke, and the search for my birth parents came to a standstill. My direction in college was a mess as well.

14. Psyched Out

I decided to major in psychology, despite witnessing electroshock therapy as an orderly. I was still enamored with Freud, Jung, and the mystery of the unconscious. Had I done my homework, I would have realized that experimental and behavioral psychology dominated the curriculum. Carl Rogers, the pioneer of humanistic psychology had taught at the University of Wisconsin from 1957-1963, and the superstar of the department now was Professor Harry Harlow, whose experiments on maternal separation and isolation (what an irony!) were important for recognizing the need for a consistent caregiver during infancy. But what he did as part of his experimental protocol was so harmful to the rhesus monkeys he experimented on that the Henry Villas Zoo in Madison placed them into a kind of rehab section after he was done with them. Harlow and his protocols later fell into disrepute.

I stayed in the Psych Department long enough to write a senior thesis on dreams and the new science of sleep. I even found a way to cite Freud and Jung in my discussion section. But I had a problem about taking the last class I needed to complete my major—advanced statistical methods. As far as I was concerned, this was irrelevant to my interests in the broader field of psychology, and it led to a showdown with an assistant dean who would not let me take an alternative course. I thought his position ridiculous and—perhaps following Mr. G's lead—I refused to take statistics and walked out his office and the program. I had drawn the line and was okay with that.

So, I switched majors to English. It was a bonus that the English Department faculty were politically aligned with the faculties in the departments of History, Sociology, and Political Science. They were all politically correct Lefties. I had found a home at last.

My love affair with the English Department was torrid but brief. I took a heavy load of English classes and received straight A's. I also accelerated my pace for graduating by taking two summer programs in English literature. The first was a travel/study program at Cambridge University in England. Morning classes were at King's College, and we had afternoons off to study or wander around the other colleges and town. It was a thrill to poke into tea shops and bookstores and walk about the shores and bridges of the River Cam. It all felt so bloody English!

We were given extra time to travel on our own, and I took one trip with friends to Wales and another on my own to Dublin. In Ireland, I hitchhiked across a small part of the countryside, where I managed to get lost while trying to bushwhack through fields and over stone walls from one village to another. This was when I realized that traveling required money, which I had little of. My short stay in Dublin, with its rich political and literary history, was thrilling. As I walked the narrow streets alone at night, I fancied myself as a young James Joyce on my way to fame. I carried a journal in my backpack, as I desperately wanted to be a writer. I was intoxicated by the romance of it all, not to mention the pints of Guinness and Harp, which I could barely afford.

At the end of the summer, our group made a quick trip to Amsterdam, where I bought some Moroccan hash and put it in my wallet—never thinking about passing through Customs in New York. Officials there seemed unconcerned that I might have $50 worth of drugs in my hip pocket, so I breezed through and soon flew home to Iowa. On the way, our airplane passed within view of downtown Chicago, where the Democratic Party Convention was being held. I was aware that protests outside the International Amphitheatre had become violent in the face of police brutality and I was peeved I wasn't there with my fellow comrades-in-arms. I was doubly frustrated, as the Woodstock Music Festival had ended only ten days earlier. Although my stay in Cambridge meant so much to me, I missed two of the most defining events of my generation in the summer of 1968.

My second summer of taking courses to gain ground on my English major requirements consisted of two classes at UCLA. This was a far less romantic experience than Cambridge and Dublin. Janelle and her friend Joyce had moved to Los Angeles for work, and I moved in with them for eight weeks in the summer of 1969.

My class on Chaucer was a nightmare. The professor, who flawlessly read passages of *The Canterbury Tales* in Old English, was brilliant but a stickler on papers and exams. I fell behind but somehow dodged a big fat F for a final grade. I had never done that poorly in a class, even including the fiasco of two semesters of calculus at Wisconsin, which was a nightmare!

By contrast, my second course at UCLA on Irish theater was a complete delight. The well-dressed, scholarly-looking older gentleman who taught it was related to the founders of the Irish

Literary Theatre in Dublin. I heard exotic accounts of the great Irish playwrights such as O'Casey and Beckett. His well-informed gossip about Shaw and Yeats was equally spell-binding. But my intellectual swoon for all things Irish was shattered by a horrific event that took place only a mile from where the two girls and I lived in East Hollywood.

News of the Tate-LaBianca murders terrified the nation, especially Los Angeles. The grotesque scene at director Roman Polanski's home was shown repeatedly on the news. Charlie Manson and his "family" were the embodiment of the worst nightmare of wild-eyed, promiscuous hippies on drugs coming to kill you. I became appropriately paranoid about my own dark beard and long hair. The stares coming my way in grocery stores and gas stations made me think everyone was wondering, *Are you one* of *them*? I kept a low profile until I drove back to Madison for the fall semester.

15. Bombed Out, Cut Out

Although research and classroom learning would be restored for periods of time, basic functions of the University of Wisconsin and university life itself were continually disrupted. There was no "normal" to return to. The campus remained in the grip of chaos and political upheaval—marked by a stream of events that changed the University, the anti-war movement, and me. These events included massive anti-war demonstrations, classroom boycotts, a Black Student Union Strike, street fighting and destruction of property, the assassinations of Martin Luther King, Jr. and Robert Kennedy, and the incursion of National Guardsmen with tanks and bayoneted rifles.

The campus closed down during three of the seven semesters I was there. President Nixon's invasion of Cambodia in the spring of 1970 turned up the heat of the anti-war movement to a boil. An even greater wave of violent demonstrations swept across hundreds of campuses and spilled onto the streets of many cities. One consequence of these protests was the increasing militancy of National Guardsmen and local police authorities, which led to the deaths of students at Kent State University in Ohio and Jackson State College in Mississippi. Following these murders, death (and the urge for revenge) were in the air in Madison.

The years of demonstrations and violence in the wake of LBJ and McNamara's escalation of the war came to a jolting halt in Madison on August 24, 1970. At 3:42 a.m., the Army Math Research Center, housed in Sterling Hall on campus, was ripped apart by a huge bomb, killing a post-doctoral student. Parts of the truck that held the plastic explosives were later found on top of an eight-story building three blocks away. The explosion damaged twenty-six other buildings and was heard ten miles away. The scope of violence and death of the student (ironically, an opponent of the war) halted the anti-war movement in its tracks in Madison, Berkeley, Columbia, and at all other major universities. After the bombing, Madison was flooded with FBI agents. Anti-war demonstrations simply ceased. Well-known radical leaders went into hiding. Students walking across campus talked in hushed voices and kept their heads down. The machinery of a new semester began to churn again, but slowly. Academic life on campus may have looked as if things had returned to normal, but they hadn't. The crater in the center of campus and the death of Robert Fassnacht told us all that nothing would ever be the same.

Four young men were charged with the bombing and death. I knew a little of two of them, who were brothers. Another was a member of the UW Crew Team and a sports writer for the *Daily Cardinal* student newspaper. The fourth was casual friend of mine. We were part of a small affinity group that prowled Madison's streets after dark following the Cambodia invasion. We became improvisational provocateurs—setting fires and erecting barricades in the streets, harassing cops, and doing minor damage to buildings, on and off campus.

Our malicious misdemeanors had been more like street theater than felonious vandalism. Despite this, when word went out that my friend was named as a co-conspirator in the bombing, many of us were in a state of disbelief. We had no idea how deep he had been in the most militant, underground faction of the anti-war movement in Madison. This was serious stuff, which led to the capture and imprisonment of all but one of them—the sports writer, Leo Burt. Despite years of being posted on the FBI's "Most Wanted" list, he has never been caught. Renderings of his likeness, were he alive today in his seventies, can still be found on the FBI's list of fugitives who remain at-large. If he has survived all these years, I wonder what his life has been like? Would a few years in prison have offered a better alternative to a lifetime on the lam—constantly on the lookout?

Today, I better see the seductive power that led us to romanticize the anti-war movement. The actions we took seemed heroic and the tactics we employed seemed justified. But even at the time, I quietly began to question how much effect we were actually having and how much collateral damage we were creating. Not only did we make enemies of the government and the military, we alienated major segments of society. Did we help light the fuse for the culture wars we're still fighting today? If so, this was a steep price to pay for doing what we thought was right.

After the bombing of the Army-Math Research Center, I was relieved to resume work for my major in English. Hefty reading assignments and papers for English classes were fun. I was hooked by Professor Sullivan and his course on modern poetry and imagism. For my official senior thesis, I wrote about the poem "The Red Wheel Barrow" by William Carlos Williams. To this day, I am amazed by this simple poem and its monumental impact on modern American poetry. But my enthusiasm was short-lived, as I had one semester until early graduation in February 1971.

I couldn't imagine getting a real job as an English major. What would I do? I certainly wasn't going home to Iowa.

I don't clearly recall why I wanted to become a high school teacher. The influence of Mr. G was an obvious piece of the puzzle. He was everything I'd hoped I could be: well-read, smart, funny, and with the guts to stand up to authority. He connected on a heart level with his students, especially those who lacked the opportunities for a better future. I was also influenced by A. S. Neill, author of *Summerhill: A Radical Approach to Child Rearing*, a book that stands in my mind as a manifesto-of-sorts for progressive education in the British tradition of child-centered schools.

This particular brand of progressive education had made its way to the US in the early 1960s, where it helped coalesce a small but enthusiastic cadre of advocates. These advocates, myself included, began promoting alternative and open-concept schools in both public and private school settings. At Summerhill School in Suffolk, England, students learned at their own pace and were encouraged to follow the path of their own learning interests, rather than be made to take a sequence of required subjects by grade level. Summerhill was also renowned for its classroom meetings and emphasis on self-government, in which students expressed their opinions and upheld rules of their own making. These precepts were not only conceptually appealing but eminently doable. Neill showed by word and example that there was another way to do schooling.

No private schools in Madison offered a progressive experience, so I'd have to teach in a public-school setting, which meant I would need a teaching credential. I had qualms about public schools, but I thought if I became an English teacher in a high school, I could marry my love of literature with a regular paying job. I was also having a pang of "radical's remorse." I felt our efforts to change the establishment from the outside were not going well; maybe I could help change the system from within. I plowed through the necessary teacher education courses and was ready to student teach in the Racine Unified School District in the spring semester.

All UW-Madison student teachers were required to meet their master teachers (supervising mentors) before school in the fall, and then attend a dinner sponsored by the local Elks Club. Knowing I had to look the role, I cut my hair, shaved my beard, and pulled out an old sports coat for the dinner. After talking at length with my master teacher, Mr. Harrison, I knew we would get along well. Student teaching beside him promised to be a great learning experience. He seemed deeply familiar with a rich portfolio of American novels and poetry. He was enthusiastic about teaching, and he was a sweet guy to boot. The dinner was pretty typical. Twosomes of student teachers were placed at tables with several Elks Club members. From a distance, we appeared to be having amiable chats with our hosts, avoiding any reference to wild demonstrations on the Madison campus. I left Racine thinking I had found my groove at last, perhaps my real calling.

Two mornings later in Madison, I received a phone call from my student teaching supervisor: "Steve, I have some rather distressing news I must share with you. Just about everybody was impressed with you, and your master teacher is eager to have you on board in the spring. The problem is that one of the Elks Club members thought you looked a little too … hippie-ish. The Elks Club believes it is proper for its student teachers to look like members of the community, not the campus in Madison. The Elks Club has been a good partner with us, so I'm afraid I must ask you to get your hair cut much shorter and shave your mustache before you return to Racine."

Neither of us said a word, as I could feel my blood pressure rise. I struggled to know what to say next. I don't recall my response verbatim, but it was something like this: "Do you mean to tell me that one Elks Club member has more say in this than my master teacher or you?" Summoning all the restraint I could muster, I told my supervisor in so many words that the Elks Club of Racine, Wizz-káhn-sen, could kiss my ass! I was quitting the program, for her lack of support for me and for not having a spine. My anger then ramped up a notch, ready to explode with another salvo of righteous indignation—which I did after she told me she was very sorry but the issue was out of her hands.

There was no doubt I had a big chip on my shoulder. I didn't like being told what I could or could not do. My buttons were easily pushed when it came to rigid authority. I rarely let out my anger, but on this occasion, I was a mad dog off its leash.

What I couldn't admit to myself at the time was that my heart was broken by not student teaching with Mr. Harrison. There was so much *animus* and anxiety to contend with on campus, I knew I had become hardened and bitter. The student teaching opportunity would have connected me to something bright and positive in my soul. It was an opportunity I was really looking forward to. And now that hope was dashed by some anonymous Elks Club guy. I was cut off from becoming a teacher, admittedly by my own hand. But there was a principle at stake, much like knowing what side of the picket line to choose. Still, this rejection stung.

I had little awareness at the time that my angry response was also triggered by the key losses and rejections in my life, starting with adoption and the painful end of my athletic future. My experiences of separation and abandonment were closely tied, and underlying them all was the fear of being invisible, not being seen, listened to, or understood. As George Orwell wrote in *1984*, "Perhaps one did not want to be loved so much as to be understood."

These impulses are powerfully held in the unconscious. They are "primitive agonies," as named by British pediatrician and psychoanalyst D.W. Winnicott, as they represent the deep and nameless qualities of suffering that result from early childhood trauma. This kind of trauma is not limited to physical or sexual abuse. It can be caused by emotional insecurity, neglect, degradation, and abandonment—both physical and psychic.

When these kinds of wounds from childhood are triggered, we may react disproportionally with strong feelings of anger, anxiety, or worthlessness. Under the duress of trauma, current or past, the body impels us to either fight or flee to protect ourselves from more suffering. We also may defend ourselves or withdraw by hiding or creating a false self that appears happy on the outside. In such a state of dissociation, it impossible to connect with others. Over the course of a lifetime, the consequences can be devastating. In the words of Jungian analyst and early childhood trauma specialist Donald Kalsched, "An infant or young child who is abused, violated, or seriously neglected by a caretaking adult is overwhelmed by intolerable affects that are impossible for it to metabolize, much less understand or even think about."[5]

Although I erupted in anger on the phone with the student teaching supervisor, my grander strategy was flight. I moved to Seattle, imagining I would become a professor of English literature specializing in modern poetry. I enrolled in the University of Washington Master's degree program in American literature, employing what Jungian analyst and author James Hollis calls the "Seattle Solution." He means that we move as far away as we can from what we want to flee: home, school, or relationships. Seattle is about as far as you can get in the contiguous United States. Hollis gets a big laugh at this quip from audiences of psychotherapists, especially in Seattle.

16. A Lesson in Synchronicity

I arrived alone in Seattle in September 1971, knowing no one. I slept in my van for a week before finding a one-room apartment across the street from the university, which had only a small desk and a straight back chair. I shared a bathroom and kitchen with five other students who were wholly uninterested in speaking with me beyond passing pleasantries. I used my sleeping bag and pad as my bed on the floor. My bookshelf and stereo cabinet were made of cheap particleboard and cinderblocks. When I was not in one of my very dull graduate seminars, I used a vacant, padded wrestling room at the University's Intramural Activities Building to do yoga and meditation. At night, I wandered into any of the nearby anomalous bars on "The Ave" to sample Rainier and Olympia Beer. Even alcohol could not take the edge off my loneliness.

I spent my first academic quarter at the University of Washington like an orphan—disconnected from my environment and myself. Bob Dylan's classic "Like a Rolling Stone" became my personal theme song; its key lyrics became my mantra for this very depressed, alone time in my life. "How does it feel, how does it feel? To be without a home, like a complete unknown, like a rolling stone?"

I felt completely out of place in the University of Washington English Department graduate program. The curriculum seemed hopelessly steeped in pre-twentieth century works. Some of the faculty looked that old to me, too. The incoming class was enormous, the largest English Department in the nation. Years later, after serving as a faculty member at three universities, I learned that high admission rates are part of an unspoken business plan for a university. High numbers at the Masters level, many of whom would drop out before completing doctoral work, paid for the salaries of tenured faculty and small class sizes for doctoral students.

Just as I had failed to do my due diligence about Carl Rogers at Wisconsin, I arrived too late at the University of Washington to study with one of the great American poets who had been a faculty member of the English Department. Theodore Roethke had died in 1963, ironically on Bainbridge Island, where I now live.

As the winter quarter of 1972 began, I roomed in a house near campus with three female grad students. Kate, also in the English Department and later my girlfriend; Christine, niece of famed psychologist Robert Yerkes, a name I knew well from Wisconsin, was in one of the science departments; and Deborah Stipek, who was in the Department of Psychology studying child development. She became a highly respected scholar in her field and eventually was named Dean of the Graduate School of Education at Stanford. We rediscovered each other at an educational research conference many years later and shared laughs and memories about living in the same house in Seattle. I recalled her as uptight, going to bed early, and running around the kitchen in an old bathrobe with pin curlers festooning her head. She remembered me staying up late, smoking dope in my room, and making loud groaning noises with Kate. Both snapshots were close to true. What was true is that I was aimless and lost—fumbling in an existential haze doing stupid things, as people and circumstances appeared and reappeared like road signs keeping me on my path.

Soon after I dropped out of graduate school, my best friend Jamie convinced me to drive a thousand pounds of Mexican marijuana in a rental car from Austin, Texas to Iowa City. I wore a cheap wig to disguise my long hair in case I got pulled over by the cops. Our income from the drug deal would support the two of us and our other hometown best friend, nicknamed Brighto, for months in the hidden recesses of western Colorado. Fortunately, I didn't get busted, but I came close. Ten hours into the trip, in the middle of a blizzard, I pulled into an all-night diner and gas station in rural southwest Missouri. To my sphincter-choking horror, a dozen highway patrolmen and local deputy sheriffs were sitting at the counter. Even they wouldn't drive in a freak storm like this! When I burst through the front entry door, snow blowing up my backside, they swiveled in unison and stared me down. I felt like a gangster being X-ray visioned by Superman. I could almost read their lips. "Well, lookee here, whadda we got?!"

I paid for my gas in cash quickly and left the change on the counter. I skipped getting anything to eat or drink, even though I was famished, and high-tailed it out of there to Iowa City, completely riveted on the icy highway and abandoned vehicles. By the grace of some holy power or guardian angel, I managed to get out of that jam. Jamie sold the dope in Iowa City for $20,000— our nest egg for Colorado!

The second story of those days is a bit different. Jamie, Brighto, and I had survived a winter in Marble, Colorado. Marble, population 40, is at the base of huge mountainside quarries. Far above town, these quarries are the source of marble used for various monuments in Washington, DC. Native lore has it that the local Ute tribe cursed the Marble Valley to prevent the white man from finding success there. Indeed, many developers' efforts to convert the slopes and valley into a ski resort have failed. The only bad luck we encountered was a septic system that froze up for a month, clogging our toilets with wretched effluent. Otherwise, we were party headquarters, inviting friends to stay with us for days or weeks. Along with gorgeous walks in the snow, our sources of entertainment were food, drink, smoke, and music. Brighto and I shared cooking duties, specializing in recipes from *Diet for a Small Planet,* by Frances Moore Lappé. My healthy way of counter-balancing the health food was the apple pie and hand-cranked ice-cream I became known for making.

As the winter of 1972-73 came to a close, we made a quick trip in my Ford Econoline van to Boulder to see friends and restock supplies. We decided to camp out one night on the way. It was still plenty cold and it got dark early. As we began to search for a state campground, we saw a lonely hitchhiker thumbing for a ride. He was about our age and traffic on the highway was sparse. We knew he'd be in trouble if we didn't take him with us. We had two tents, an extra sleeping bag, and plenty of food. He was happy to accept our invitation to join us for the night. We had a grand time. I made vegetarian stew with rice in a large camp pot. We had enough Coors beer for all. After dinner, Jamie pulled out some killer weed called "The One." The four of us got so incredibly high off that one joint, I thought we were actually flying around the campfire, soaring through the tree tops to the sky. We were hallucinating for sure. That night we laughed so hard that we thought our guts would explode out of our mouths. That dope was not called The One for nothing. Soon after we'd packed up in the morning and headed to Boulder, our new friend asked to be let off at the next intersection, as he was going on to Grand Junction. After he jumped out, he handed me a long, narrow pouch made of suede leather.

He looked straight at me and said, "I just want to thank you again for your hospitality. You guys are something special. I will never forget you and I will certainly not forget The One!" He asked if I knew what yarrow sticks were. I said I didn't. He then asked if I knew what the *I Ching* was. I said I had heard of it, but wasn't familiar with it.

He told me, "You use these yarrow sticks to get a reading. They form a hexagram that will have a special meaning just for you. Go to Boulder Book Store and buy a book called *I Ching* by Wilhelm—that's Richard Wilhelm not Hoyt Wilhelm the baseball player. The book will explain the hexagram's meaning. Good luck!" With that he quickly turned and made his way to the other side of the highway, where he flagged down an oncoming pickup truck for a ride. It was all so sudden. He was there and then he was gone.

In Boulder that afternoon, I went to the book store and found the *I Ching or Book of Changes* by Richard Wilhelm, with its classic gray cover with yellow lettering. I purchased it and hurried back to the house where we were staying. Interestingly, that house, north of the Hotel Boulderado, was once owned by physicist Robert Oppenheimer, who became head of the Manhattan Project in Los Alamos, New Mexico in 1942. As we all know, the physicists of the Manhattan Project developed the atomic bomb, which was used to destroy two large cities in Japan in 1945. Oppenheimer's old house had a musty smell to it, and it reminded me of the scorched artifacts from wartime Japan at home.

With my copy of the *I Ching* in hand, I leapt into the somewhat complicated instructions on how to manipulate the yarrow sticks. The English translation of Wilhelm's German text is not an easy read, as Wilhelm faithfully stuck to the six line-by-line classic interpretation for each of the sixty-four hexagrams. I threw the sticks, which organized into a representation of Hexagram #50 – The Cauldron.

My takeaway from Wilhelm's commentary was that the cauldron symbolizes nourishment and rejuvenation, as though taken from a cooking pot. It also stands for breakthrough, transformation, and fulfilling one's destiny. But like cooking food in a pot or a cauldron, one must exercise patience. If one can learn to stand the heat of the fire, one can allow oneself to be like an empty vessel for the good of all.

Whether I actually understood the nuances of Wilhelm's commentary was secondary to the feeling that fell over me. I was learning a new way of seeing—interpreting hexagrams in a way that was true only for me in only that moment. It seemed to signal a new beginning, and a calling to nourish and serve others. Fate was in my favor. I felt this was a call to get back on my path and embrace a new challenge such as teaching in the spirit of A. S. Neill and *Summerhill*. My response to the *I Ching* was to bid adieu to my buddies once our lease expired and head back to the Pacific Northwest.

But there was more to my reading of Wilhelm. As I flipped through the pages, to my great surprise I found that the foreword was by C.G. Jung. Jung described that in his initial encounter with the *I Ching,* he also drew #50 – The Cauldron. I was stunned that I had the same reading as Jung on my first try. As I read further, Jung explained that the mindset for reading the *I Ching* required that we dispense with our singular belief in causality. Rather, the *I Ching* embraced seeming coincidence and the "immense importance of chance." For Jung, understanding the *I Ching*

> involves a certain curious principle that I have termed *synchronicity,* a concept that formulates a point of view diametrically opposed to causality.... [S]ynchronicity takes the coincidence of events in space and time as meaning something more than mere chance, namely a peculiar interdependence of objective events among themselves as well as subjective (psychic) states of the observer or observers.[6]

I was not all that familiar with Jung at the time, but it struck me that the so-called coincidence of receiving yarrow sticks from a stranger and drawing the same hexagram as he had on my first attempt was beyond uncanny. Oddly coincidental too was that just the night before, I had fed our camping group a stew made in a large pot. That dinner was the prelude to a great night of fun under the protective canopy of giant Colorado pines. I thought back to my early encounters with Jung, reading *Man and His Symbols* as a teenager and citing him in my senior psychology thesis. It was all too much for me to take in—too coincidental to be understood logically.

My first conscious experience with synchronicity was a doozy! Jung and synchronicity opened up a different way for me to understand life, or at least get a glimmer of what lay behind the veil of everyday reality. My experience with the *I Ching* felt like a gift; and through it, I felt a distinct nudge to get on with my life.

Today the term *synchronicity* has nearly become jargon. Even in some Jungian circles, its meaning has lapsed into a prosaic synonym for coincidence and serendipity. Learning about synchronicity from books and lectures is one thing. Learning it straight from that experience in Colorado was quite another. I think

71

my return to Seattle can be understood as a call to move beyond learning from books. It was an invitation, perhaps a mandate, to jump into the fray of life—gritty, messy, and confusing.

As I prepared to leave for the Northwest, I knew I could stay with my girlfriend when I arrived. Beyond that, I didn't have much of a plan, only a call, like a whisper of wind gently rustling through Aspen trees. I had a faint vision of one day starting a school that would not be like the others. I trusted my vision; it felt authentic and possible. I wanted to create a school where I could be me and not have to shave or wear a sports coat. I concurred wholeheartedly with Henry David Thoreau when he proclaimed, "Beware of all enterprises that require new clothes." Returning to Seattle would be a new chapter in my life. I knew I was on my way to meet or make my destiny.

PART FOUR

When the student is ready, the teacher appears.
When the student is truly ready, the teacher disappears.
~ Lao Tzu, Sixth-Century Chinese philosopher ~

17. Just Jump In

My vision of myself as the Don Quixote of progressive education faded as quickly as the doomed SST. Beginning in 1969, Seattle's Boeing Company, after a decade of rapid growth in air travel, began laying off employees due to oversaturation of the airplane market. The company was on the verge of bankruptcy when, in 1971, the US government cut funding to the company's Supersonic Transport (SST) program. The "Boeing Bust" triggered massive unemployment statewide, which led to collective dysphoria. A local billboard bemoaning the times read: "Would the last person leaving SEATTLE – please turn out the lights?"

Enrollment in Seattle's public schools had been in freefall for five years, and hundreds of teachers had been laid off. There were very few jobs available. I was nearly broke, and were it not for Kate taking me in, I would have returned to Iowa with my tail between my legs. But something prompted me to stay. I knew I had to make something of myself or stay invisible forever.

I had little going for me at the time, other than living with a woman as a couple for the first time. Kate had a job at a social-policy think tank, which provided us a margin of security beyond the food stamps I received from the state. Taking education courses at the University of Washington during the day and working the graveyard shift at Harborview Hospital was a grind. I was so sleep-deprived I felt stoned much the time—as though on a steady IV-drip of "The One."

I had been foolhardy to bet on a career in education. I was a little arrogant too, as I thought I could play the system in my favor once I had a teaching credential. But I still believed in my vision, perhaps more out of desperation than inspiration. And so, I lobbied hard to get a teaching assignment at one of the Seattle School District's alternative schools, and my diligence paid off. My University of Washington academic supervisor regarded me with suspicion, as these were schools that no other prospective teachers wanted to be placed in.

I was notified that I would be student teaching at Sanislo Elementary in West Seattle. It wasn't an alternative school per se, as it also served as a regular neighborhood school. But spatially and programmatically it was a genuine open concept school, where students learn in ways suited to their individual interests and teachers work collaboratively in teams. There were four hundred students in one gigantic classroom, in multi-aged groupings. As ginned-up as I was on progressive schooling, I had to set aside all that I knew. I leapt blindly into what turned out to be one of the best experiences of my career in education.

I arrived at Sanislo on a Monday morning in early September 1974 for an initial chat with Principal Phil McCloskey. I was well-groomed, as I didn't want to repeat the run-in I'd had with the Racine Elks Club. My hair was trimmed, although I kept my mustache, and I wore a presentable sports coat without a tie. That was the last time I wore a sports coat in a school until I became a principal a decade later. Phil was wearing a checkered shirt, khaki pants, and low-cut hiking boots.

The conversation was short. Phil told me I wasn't going to have a master teacher to work with, and that I'd be working with a fourth through sixth grade team. Without further ado, he led me out of his office, motioned in the general direction of the large center room, and said, "Your team meets in the far corner. They'll teach you what to do. Don't worry, just jump in," and he vanished.

So I walked to the end of the office corridor, turned a corner to find my team, and wham!—the roar of four hundred kids rolled over me like a tsunami. I saw a topsy-turvy tidal wave of human bodies of all shapes, sizes, and colors: black, brown, white, and multiple shades between. Kids were *everywhere!* Some were doing artwork in small groups, some sat one-on-one with a teacher, some were in large groups listening to books being read aloud, and some sequestered themselves on couches and were reading all by themselves.

I loped over rivers of kids to find the adults I thought were likely to be my new teammates. Their welcome was cordial but brief. They were, after all, teaching. "Just hang out today and watch. Tomorrow you can jump in." There was that phrase again: *jump in.*

It was clear that although I was a member of a team, I needed to learn to teach and survive on my own. The lessons I needed weren't in books. The teachers didn't even seem to have lesson plans. I had to learn by watching, asking, and trying things out. I knew that if I was ever going to be good teacher, I had to become a good listener and observer, and get over myself fast. At the end of each day, I was exhausted, but my vision for starting a school slowly began to come into focus.

Most important, I got used to feeling in over my head, figuring out how to both teach and discipline children. My teammates—three women and a man—showed me the way. The commotion of an open concept school just rolled off them. In time, the clatter and chaos rolled off me too, as I lost the need to know what should happen next.

Gary Burdge, my one male teaching colleague, and I hit it off from the start. We shared our professional dreams and what we believed could be an innovative school model—even more radical than Sanislo. Because of the district's financial crisis and cuts in the work force, Gary wasn't sure he'd be working there next year, as his seniority ranking was low. If Gary were to be laid off, it would surely spell doomsday for me. Nevertheless, we continued our discussions and dreamed aloud that someday we might teach together, perhaps starting our own alternative school in Seattle.

My time at Sanislo was indeed brief. Nevertheless, in this time I was part of the staff, participated in staff birthday parties, showers, and holiday functions. I was surprised how raunchy some of our festivities got, as Phil, Gary, and I were the only men in the group. At the Christmas White Elephant gift exchange, the male porn star playing cards was the most sought-after gift by the female staff. Our holiday hoopla was over the top.

At Sanislo, I saw what was possible, not just in school design and philosophy, but in the lives of teachers and students. However, day-to-day life was not one big love-fest. The kids could be very tough. There were fights and bold-faced acts of defiance. On several occasions, a parent barged into the school looking to settle a score with a teacher or threaten another kid from the neighborhood. Teachers were not always of one mind. There were tensions over how much freedom we should give the kids, and how much structure and discipline we should impose. Cliques and rivalries formed within the staff. Phil seemed to know when to interject himself, when to adjudicate, and when to back off. I learned from him to distinguish problems that could be solved from dilemmas that could only be managed. What I witnessed was a judicious interpersonal skillset, which I knew was requisite for leadership in any setting.

My short tenure at Sanislo spoiled me, as nothing would surpass the thrill of learning so much so quickly, and feeling so connected with a like-minded group of professionals. As in the Frank Capra movie *Lost Horizon*, once I left Sanislo—my Shangri-La—I could never find my way back again. But what I took from Sanislo lasted a lifetime.

I've always believed that my encounter with the *I Ching* and synchronicity in Boulder led me to Sanislo, which then served as the cauldron of my learning. Green as I was, my new professional identity was forged there. The call to create a unique school and become a leader was my destiny.

Through it all, I never forgot the mystery of my adoption, and it wasn't long before my inquiries began anew. I was being pulled in two directions—the question of my identity as an adopted child and the quest toward a career as school innovator and leader. Through my career, I was beginning to take control of my life. But as John Lennon said, "Life is what happens to you while you're busy making other plans." In the coming years, fate commandeered my life elsewhere.

18. ORCA

Gary called me with the bad and good news. The bad news was that he had been laid off and would not be at Sanislo next year. The good news was that the Seattle Teachers Association (our union) might get some jobs back. There were openings at the Allen Free School near Green Lake, a perfect alternative school for him. He thought it was likely he'd be able to transfer there, and wondered if the same might be true for me. "If I can get a place there, maybe you could go for the other opening. You'd be perfect, and we can finally teach together."

I expressed my profound doubt, but when school opened in the fall, the second position at the Allen Free School was still open. They could find no one with seniority who had an alternative school philosophy that would fit. So, with a flurry of paperwork, delays, interviews, and more delays, I finally got the job. Gary and I would co-teach two multi-age groups in rooms across the hallway from each other. I was elated. My time had arrived!

We agreed to quietly redesign the program on our own. The three veteran teachers who helped found the Free School were not keen about our ideas, as we had much less teaching experience than they did. But we persisted. Their program was stale, deeply enmeshed in a fuzzy, laissez-faire philosophy. The school's climate was chaotic, as anyone passing by an open classroom window could tell. Some days it felt like the kids ran the school in the name of being *free*. It was no surprise the kids weren't learning much. The school lacked the cohesion of Sanislo. The Free School's teachers were understandably exhausted and ineffective. Gary and I were cocky enough to think we had a solution, but it would take several years for us to be successful.

Our energy and originality eventually trumped their inertia. We laid out a comprehensive curriculum, which went beyond the basic skills. Our proposal included the arts, dance, yoga, oceanography, athletics (running), cooking, and book making. With the exception of the veteran kindergarten teacher, who would never change her ways, we won over (or cajoled) our colleagues into a vision of a new program. The parents were enthusiastic as well. I think they liked the idea that their kids would have more structure and accountability, which probably was lacking at home. In time it worked well. It was a labor of love—a lot of labor and a lot of love.

Along the way, we changed the school's name to ORCA, in honor of ocean explorer Jacques Cousteau. Gary had been so inspired by Cousteau that he choreographed a Whale Dance for the kids to perform in public in his honor. At its heart, the Whale Dance was about saving the whales, which was a popular cause at the time. The dance became well-known and helped garner attention to the program. Because of our local fame, we got a little extra staffing from the school district, which gave Gary more time to develop curriculum and allowed me the flexibility to become the school's administrative liaison. I was living my dream. Our vision was becoming a reality.

During those early years of becoming a teacher, I hadn't seen much of my family in Iowa. I relied on phone calls with Mom to catch up, especially regarding Dad's struggle with ALS. He had long since lost his ability to walk and talk, and was now completely bedridden and received nourishment only through a tube. Mom had renewed her license as a Registered Nurse to help with his round-the-clock care at Burlington Hospital.

As with most ALS victims, his muscles had atrophied. The only means of communication was a lettered Ouija board that he used with a pointer in his mouth to spell out words. At the end, he was left only with his eye lids subtly motioning in one direction or another to communicate a yes or no to her questions. Mom could intuit his words and feelings by reading his eye movements. This was a staggeringly tragic and miraculous thing to watch between them. As for my mother, this was her finest hour. For all the rancor that had erupted between us over the years, an unexpected truce broke out. Old grudges went away. As she quit worrying about minutiae, her anxiety subsided and her disposition sweetened. I feel sad today that I never told her then how I admired her steadfast care of Dad in his last years.

I returned home at Christmas break. One evening I sat alone with Dad in his hospital room. After an hour of thinking up new things to talk about, I quit trying and just sat with him in silence. How easy it would be for me to end it all for him, to put him out of his misery. For all I knew, he might have wanted me to put a pillow over his face and gently suffocate him. He could offer no resistance whatsoever. I would have done that for him. But then again, with Mom in mind, I couldn't. It wasn't my call to make. It was hers, and I respected her right to do what she thought was best.

I returned to the hospital to say goodbye to him before I flew back to Seattle. With Mom at my side, I kissed his forehead and told him I loved him. I stood quietly for a moment, knowing this was the last time I would see him alive. My heart broke as I looked at him lying motionless in his hospital bed, staring blankly at the ceiling without a motion or a sound. I had no way to know if he could see or hear me. He was locked in the prison of his own body. I could not begin to imagine the condition of his mind, let alone his soul. I knew his death would come soon, though, and when it did, it would be a blessing for us all.

The call came a few months later. I was at ORCA in a morning classroom meeting with my third and fourth grade students. Before I picked up the phone in the school office, I knew. A family member told me Dad had died last night. To me, and I think to the rest of the family, this was a bittersweet moment. He had struggled and suffered for seven years. Everyone in the family had said their goodbyes. We were now in a state of silent relief. Yet, I felt a deep sadness—a soft and mournful feeling that remains in my soul to this day. Dad, more than Mom, showed a quality of faith and patience in me that few parents would have offered to a son who was determined to live a life different from theirs. They had expected me to be a doctor, like Dad, but I didn't comply. I knew that being a physician was not my destiny.

Dad had good reasons to worry about me, but if that were the case, he never showed it. If not for him, who knows what I would have become? At age twenty-nine, I was teaching kids with valued colleagues in the school of my dreams. I think Dad saw the renegade streak in me, and he let me become me. What greater blessing can a parent give a child? Who could be so lucky as to have a man like him adopt me as his son?

As I walked back to the classroom that morning, the students knew something was up. I told them that there was no one else I would rather be with right now. It was my good fortune to be with them in this moment. As I closed my eyes to weep, I could hear the students rise. I could feel their small, warm bodies tighten around mine, and for a moment, I felt we had merged together as one simple and sorrowful breath. I stood motionless in their midst, as I felt more love surge through me than I could possibly hold.

* * *

My adoption issues were still with me. Before Dad died, I wrote to the American Home Finding Service again, and this time the response was from a new director, Mr. Tom Lazio. His letter, dated April 28, 1975, contained reminders about the restrictions of legally sealed records, but his tone was different from that of Mr. C. W. O'Rourke. Lazio wrote at length to empathize with my situation. Then he really surprised me and asked for my help.

> I would appreciate some correspondence with you and would request permission from you to use your inquiry as typical of the kinds of concerns we receive from adopted children....I feel like this kind of educational process could do a lot in working with the Board members and the general public at large to make them more aware of the void in your background and the uncertainty you have lived with for years.

Three years later, in early 1978, I wrote to him again. His reply arrived a few weeks before Dad died. He reiterated that the previous director had probably erred in giving me more information than he was legally entitled to. I had a passing pang of guilt for judging C.W. O'Rourke so harshly. But I found the new director to be genuinely compassionate, as well as direct. Lazio wrote (dated February 15, 1978):

> I hope you could understand that your biological parents made the decision at the time that it would be better for you to be adopted than try to raise you under the circumstances of their relationship, namely being unmarried and unable to make the commitment to you as parents that they felt was essential. I agree with you that you did not

have any choice in the matter ... [but] parents are
often confronted with decisions that affect their
children and have far reaching impact on their
lives. Sometimes those decisions have to be made
with limited information.

I met Tom Lazio many years later, and the impression I
got from him then was the same as I'd had from his letters. His
tone was warm and understanding, and his words of advice felt
authentic and not condescending. I was flattered that he wanted
me to write a letter to an Iowa State Senate committee that was
reviewing the laws about sealed adoption records. He seemed
determined to help ease those restrictions; he was on my side. My
follow-up letter up to Mr. Lazio would not be the last time I would
express my appreciation to him.

A lot of other important things stirred in my life after
Dad died. Kate and I bought an old farmhouse just north of the
University. She soon worked at ORCA, too, as we shared my
teaching job while I was doing administrative work. We even co-
taught a human sexuality class, which was a bit unconventional
for its time, as she was an ardent feminist. But the fifth graders
and their parents seemed to like what we were doing. If we tried
to teach that class today, I'm sure some MAGA mob would take
after us.

During these years, my interest in Buddhism began to
blossom, as I was drawn to the dharma by Chögyam Trungpa
Rinpoche's book *Cutting Through Spiritual Materialism*. Trungpa,
a Tibetan former monk, had moved from Canada in 1971 to
found the Shambhala Community in Boulder. Two of my former
classmates were part of that community, and I learned a lot
from their journey into Buddhism. I was far from wanting to
make a commitment like theirs. Still, they encouraged my interest
and recommended other teachers and schools of Buddhism.
My evolving spiritual awareness eventually led me to teachers

like Adyashanti and Shunryu Suzuki Roshi, and practices like meditation and Zen kōans.

As my interest in Buddhism grew, my restlessness began to stir again. I don't think one caused the other, but their confluence felt like synchronicity. I had accomplished what I'd set out to do at ORCA. I helped design and lead a school program. Now I was ready to master another set of skills and dream another vision. I was hungry for more learning. I could not yet admit that I was also ready to move on without Kate. Whatever the cause of eagerness for a new life journey, I could feel the restlessness roiling away in my cauldron.

Soon, I knew that I was ready to go back to graduate school. I also knew it would have to be somewhere special—someplace that was authentic and would challenge me. I didn't really need much coaxing to consider Stanford. A parent of one of my ORCA students had been admitted to the Graduate School of Education there the prior year. I trusted her judgment and encouragement, although I already knew this was the only place I wanted to go. But I was anything but confident about getting in or doing well there.

My undergrad grades were pretty good, but not stellar. I knew I needed to do really well on the Graduate Record Examinations (GRE) if I were to have a chance of getting in. When I opened the envelope with my scores, I was blown away to find a 700 (out of 800) for the quantitative (math) section. I had bombed calculus in college. But that was then, and this was my future. *California, here I come!*

19. Stanford – *Yo Sé Quién Soy*

Attending Stanford was another dream come true. The campus and surrounding foothills were breathtaking in their beauty. Everything at Stanford was first-class. I knew the academic challenges would be enormous, even scary; but what I couldn't foresee was that my professors, and others I encountered while conducting interviews for my dissertation, would have a more lasting impact on me than my coursework. And that's saying a lot, as I learned so much from each class.

The Graduate School of Education's welcoming ceremony for incoming students was led by Dean Mike Atkin. Angst filled the room, especially when a number of famous faculty members filed in the back of the auditorium to check us out. The mood shifted quickly, however, when the Dean told us: "You've already jumped through the hoops. Getting in was the hard part. Now, there is nothing more to prove. Roll up your sleeves. It's time to get to work."

He went on to say that during the first year, we would not be assigned to write long research papers. In fact, all of our papers would be limited to three pages, double-spaced. This was welcome news, indeed! But as I began to write three-page papers in the first month, I realized just how hard it is to be limited to three pages. It reminded me of the old trope attributed to Mark Twain. "If I had more time, I would have written a shorter letter." My classmates and I quickly learned we needed a lot of time to a write a well-crafted three-page paper, making every word count.

The skill needed to write in a clean, concise style— the *Stanford Style*—was made clear to me in two rare classes I took from the former Dean of the School of Education, Dr. Art Coladarci. He was a richly interesting guy with a sense of humor that wouldn't quit. He had held the position of Academic Secretary to the Senate of the Academic Council for twenty years. His notes were legendary, as the previous meeting's notes were read aloud before each meeting—often bringing down the house for his wit and teasingly biting quips about his colleagues and the subjects of the day. He was that way in class too: witty and sharp, but gentler. Art never lectured, but he could riff endlessly on the English language, his military service in Korea, and heading up the Woodside Horse Patrol. He would spend two hours talking about the semicolon or the perils of excess verbiage. You have to be damn clever to make those subjects hilarious.

We would bring to class a portion of paper we were working on for another class. Those who were brave enough consented to have him project our work on a screen for the rest of the class (and him) to comment on. This was as much fun as surgery without an anesthetic, in full view of a large gallery of rookie surgeons. It could be brutal. We also would turn papers into him for suggested revisions. He penned his comments in red ink, so when he handed them back, they looked like someone had severed an artery on them. Through it all, I acquired a minimal level of mastery, which paid off for me. As a teaching assistant for the next three years, I graded papers for other professors. This too taught me about good writing and teaching. It also helped pay for my hefty tuition.

I was blessed to take courses from some of the great teachers and scholars of that era. My dissertation committee was an all-star lineup: Larry Cuban (Chair), Mike Kirst, and Milbrey McLaughlin, each renowned in their respective fields. Larry had been superintendent of schools in Arlington, Virginia; Mike was on the California State Board of Education and served as special advisor to Governor Jerry Brown; and Milbrey had earned her stripes at the Rand Corporation in Santa Monica. They had real-life experience outside of academe, which was especially appealing to me. I worked for each of them as a research or teaching assistant, as I had with famed education historian David Tyack. It was an honor to work for each of them. What influenced me the most were their respective blends of brilliance, authenticity, and care for their students. To this day, I find something of each of them within me.

When it came time to write my dissertation, I followed the axiom: Write about what you know. So, I wrote a case study of the history of Seattle School District in the tumultuous years during which I became a teacher at ORCA. It was a fascinating period to study, as it included the combined chaos of desegregation, financial crises, teacher unionization, school closures, and the upheaval of the traditional structures of governance and administration. This was true of other urban school districts in that period, as well.

In my third year, I moved back to Seattle from Palo Alto to conduct the research. I interviewed over fifty school board members, administrators, city officials, and parent activists of that time. Most of those I interviewed opened up to me, both on and off the record, and offered even more than I'd asked of them. Their off-the-record tales were revealing and occasionally salacious. These antecdotes were not just gossip, but important information for understanding why people acted and made decisions the ways they did. I learned of mental breakdowns, rivalries, alcoholism, and affairs that involved school district personnel and high-profile politicians and activists in the Seattle community. Of course, I didn't use embarrassing information, as it served no purpose in my case study. But it did help me understand the underbelly of any organization's culture and how much it affects its success and direction.

The most prophetic interview comment came to me as advice from David Moberly, the much-reviled Seattle Public Schools Superintendent from 1976-1980, known as the Hatchet Man for all the cuts he made to staff. He chained-smoked and talked nonstop during our interview. To my surprise, I found him to be warm and candid, even generous in appraisal of others, many of whom I knew hated him during his rocky four-year tenure. I think he sensed that I was interested in the superintendency as a long-range goal. When the two-hour interview ended, he led me to the door, put his arm around my shoulder, and proclaimed with a bit of tenderness in his voice, "Son, you're going to be a superintendent one day, I just know it. And you will be a good one, but only if you remember this one thing. They [a school board] are going to can your ass one day, whether you are good or bad. So, once you get the job, get the hell out there and do what you think is best. Fuck 'em! Get away with as much as you can until they fire your ass. If you don't, you won't be able to live with yourself."

He then lit up another cigarette and returned to his office. Something told me I should remember this parting advice. It turned out, he was right. One day, somebody did fire my ass, and by then I could live with the consequences and myself, but just barely. The Hatchet Man must have seen this in me, too.

For my dissertation, I wanted to know how and why leaders of organizations make decisions and lead in times of stress and uncertainty. In fact, I wanted to know how so many smart, well-intentioned people could act so stupidly, so counter-intuitively. I was intrigued by the *psychological* dynamics of the key players, not just their policies.

Between 1970 and 1975, the Seattle School District lost five thousand students a year, more than twenty-five percent of its student population. During that steep decline both in enrollment and state funding, not one school was closed. Why? What accounted for the breakdown of rational thought—not by one person but by a whole community? Finding the answer to that question spurred my interest in depth psychology. My curiosity about the unconscious dynamics in a person and in our collective selves only grew once my dissertation was completed.

The professor who had the most impact on me at Stanford was James G. March. Jim was a pioneer in organizational theory and organizational decision making. He coined the term "the garbage can model of decision making," which elicits an image of a virtual garbage can in which problems and solutions are thrown in and drawn out simultaneously in a nonrational, random fashion. The garbage can dynamic is the stuff of real life—full of confusion, ambiguity, and contradictions.

Jim was an impressive figure—an accomplished poet who spoke five languages and taught at universities around the world. At Stanford, he simultaneously held positions in the School of Education, the Business School, and the Hoover Institution on

War, Revolution and Peace. His résumé was a sight to behold; but as I got to know him, I found him also to be a man filled with generosity and kindness who never forgot his Midwestern roots.

His seminar on organizational theory was memorable, and scary as hell. There were two dozen students in class, half of whom held post-doctoral fellowships. The readings for the course were all over the map—literally—as they ranged from the rise and fall of the Roman Empire to the random pattern of school superintendent succession in Wisconsin to the organizational and political decision processes leading to the unification of Japan's power and utility regions. When I saw the reading list with two challenging papers we had to read for each semi-weekly seminar, I didn't think I'd survive it.

When Jim announced that the members of the class would be *teaching* these papers each week, I went into a full-on panic. A year ago, I'd been teaching fifth graders and now I would be presenting papers to guys with PhDs from the London School of Economics. Jim assigned a number to each of us for the quarter, and at the beginning of every class, he would bring a fresh printout from a random number generator and announce the order of presentations that day. Not knowing whether we'd have to make a presentation on one of these dense papers until the last minute meant we had to be thoroughly prepared for each class. Even the post-docs looked pale.

At the first seminar, Jim established two ground rules. Every class would begin with us naming which word or phrase in the paper we were about to study together we didn't know the meaning of. Hmm? No one was eager to say what he or she didn't know. Following a prolonged silence, he'd say something like, "Page two, first paragraph. "*Stochastic modeling.* Who can tell us what that means?" More silence.

"Mr. Elgin. This should be up your tree. Can you tell us what the term stochastic modeling means?"

It was agony, like a scene from the movie *The Paper Chase* with Professor Charles Kingfield grilling a hapless first-year law student. The following class, more students brought forth words they didn't understand. No one could claim they knew every term in these very dense papers.

The second rule was. "When it's your turn to present a paper, don't tell us what's wrong with it. Any jackass can do that. Tell us what's right about it!"

I could see students quickly crossing out major sections of their presentations, and reconsidering what was *right* about that particular paper. I followed suit. To my relief, Jim had a way of leveling the class over time. The smarties got taken down a notch, and people like me were buoyed by his way of encouraging us to speak without fear of criticism. In time, my confidence grew, as did my connection with him.

One day I asked to speak with him after class. I wanted to know if he would be on my dissertation committee, as I was quite sure I would use his work on nonrational decision making as a primary theoretical lens for my case study. He seemed almost flattered that I would ask him, which threw me off-guard. I was sure he was overloaded with his own students, his research, teaching duties, and so forth. He declined my request, with regret, as he said was going to be on sabbatical when I would be completing my work. Then he added, "You know, Steve, you were really good in class today."

I must have looked puzzled, so he added, "Yes. You spoke only about what you knew. In a group like this, that's rare and I admire it." I cannot remember a time, before or since, when I felt so complimented. Coming from Jim March, that pat on the back meant the world to me.

The other enduring lesson from Jim March was from a film he later wrote and narrated: *Passion and Discipline: Don Quixote's Lessons for Leadership* (2003).[7] The film, shot in Spain, was based on a course he taught on learning about leadership through literature. Although Cervantes' Quixote appears to be a counterintuitive model for leadership, he remains undeterred from his chivalric mission. He is determined to right wrongs and vanquish the enemies of justice, regardless of the consequences. Even though Quixote is seen by others as a two-bit knight and a delusional fool, his values and commitment to his calling hold steady against all circumstances. Quixote shows us, as Jim declared, that life and leadership require equal measures of passion and discipline. Leadership is about knowing who you are. It is about being able to say, as Don Quixote, *¡Yo sé quién soy!* I know who I am.

20. Mr. Smart Guy from Stanford

You might think getting a PhD from Stanford would have provided the focus and confidence to plan my next steps, but no. I was clueless, and put off any consideration of my future, telling myself I was too busy completing my dissertation to know what was next.

My love life was equally precarious. After my breakup with Kate, I was like a honeybee, flitting from one flower to the next, as though I were the card-carrying playboy I'd been in high school. My bad-boy behavior was unleashed even before Kate and I officially split. I kept secrets from her while I was away at Stanford, which was neither a healthy way to be together nor to part. I regret I didn't handle it better, for her sake and for mine.

Over time, what I wanted to do next became clear. I wanted to follow in Larry Cuban's footsteps and become a school superintendent, then a college professor. To do so, I would have to climb a career ladder, and the first rung seemed to be principalship. I wanted to work in a multicultural setting replete with Title I schools. I felt I could make a bigger difference in people's lives going into a school setting rather than sitting in an office writing policy.

I needed both a principal and superintendent internship before I could be fully licensed for either, and I found an opportunity in the Redwood City School District, eight miles north of Palo Alto. I spent the fall semester interning for a principal in a school that was 95 percent Latino. A sizable number of students had limited English skills, as many were born in Mexico or Central America.

For the spring semester, I interned with the Superintendent of the district, Dr. Ken Hill, a bright and affable man, whose charm emanated from his self-deprecating humor. I don't think there was an employee in the Redwood City School District that didn't adore and respect him. It was a special opportunity to work side-by-side with such a great superintendent. My "office" was a cramped, windowless storage closet across the hall from Ken's office. I didn't care, despite an occasional eye-roll from me at Ken's sympathetic Executive Secretary Doris.

My first and most memorable assignment was to chair the District Report Card Committee, whose task was to overhaul the outdated elementary school report card. This was my initiation to public school administration, and any insider knows that this assignment is the kiss of death. I was teased mercilessly by other administrators in the central office. Trying to make a report card committee get something done was like trying to rewrite the Constitution.

The committee majority were seasoned, highly opinionated, and mostly female teachers who were prepared to fight to the death over hot-button issues like the number and type of gradable categories for penmanship. This was at a time when cursive penmanship was on the way out and computers with keyboards were on the way in.

Their arguments were endless and fundamentally insane. Many of them had a take-no-prisoners attitude about winning their points and convincing others what a good report card should contain. If the most vocal of these committee members had their way, the report card would have been five pages long. My polite interjections calling for common sense fell on deaf ears. I lost control of the committee before I had any. To them, I was just another lackey administrative placeholder. I also learned about psychological projection in my stint as committee chair. I unwittingly served as projection screen for an ex-husband, domineering father, or ungrateful son who had wronged them in the distant or recent past. Their treatment sometimes was on the edge of being rude—Dr. Smarty Pants from Stanford. What the hell did I know, anyway?!

The only bright light of my Report Card Committee experience was meeting an attractive woman about my age who often sat at a table across from mine. When the fur was flying between factions of veteran teachers, my eyes kept wandering back to her. I couldn't help myself. I wondered if anyone noticed. Physically, she was a knock-out. Her energy was radiant and it was clear that she was popular with even her most gnarly colleagues. I learned later that her name was Johanna and her California license plate number was 5ACIOUS—so apt. Her laughter and enthusiasm were contagious. I was definitely attracted to her, but I also was in a relationship at the time, so I needed to keep my distance. I knew then our destinies would meet one day. That said, I had no idea that, eventually, she and I would get married.

It was hard to concentrate on the controversy of how to grade the skills of mathematical computation and applications, when my brain was reeling in fantasy. It was more than lust at first sight. I couldn't get her out of my mind. Fate intervened a year a later when she was assigned to work as a cooperative teaching coach at Roosevelt Elementary School, where I had become principal. This was as complicated as it was lucky, as word spread fast that I was seeing a staff member after hours.

My five years as principal at Roosevelt were typical in many respects. The job required a great deal of patience to weather the predictable turbulence of life in an elementary school.

There was much more to it than supervising children. There was the annual ritual of managing and evaluating twenty-five teachers, no easy task. There was also the care and feeding of parents and central office administrators, which required more schmoozing than ability. The most difficult task, if a school is to be well-led, was to help create a climate of collaboration; and to that end, help create a shared vision for the school and its community. To succeed, I needed to master the fine arts of persuading, cajoling, and even flattering. Eventually I also learned that not every teacher has to sign on for it to work.

It became my habit to take the staff out for drinks after the school's Open House at a wonderfully cheesy bar called The Gypsy Cellar in downtown Redwood City, complete with a violin-playing owner from Hungary. A few free drinks and some good laughs had a way of bringing us together. Our personal camaraderie allowed me to cobble together enough teachers and classified staff members to say we had a vision, a joint purpose.

But it was more than a few honed social skills that helped this happen. We were the recipients of a major grant to implement a schoolwide program in *cooperative learning*—with guess who as the cooperative learning lead coach? Johanna, of course.

This new program was a radical shift for the teachers, who were used to being kings and queens of their classrooms. Cooperative learning was not only a new way of teaching and learning, it required a new kind of collaboration among teachers. Bringing the staff together was more of a political strategy than instructional. Traditionally, teachers are trained to follow established curricula and textbooks. Deviation from the program is not only frowned upon but laborious. In many cases, getting teachers to adopt a new pedagogy was like trying to convince a card-carrying carnivore to become vegan—a tough sell. But I gradually learned to enjoy the process of slow change and the inevitable complications of introducing new ideas and innovative practices that were unwelcome at first.

When my tenure ended in 1990, I knew I had a penchant for innovation and vision. I liked the feeling of being a school leader. I admit I enjoyed the reputation I had acquired in that role. More importantly, I liked knowing I had the capacity to do even bigger things. The past twenty years had been like a learning laboratory for me, full of successes, failures, and dead-ends. I was not unscathed. But now, like Don Quixote, I was beginning to know who I was.

PART FIVE

A child who feels misunderstood by his biological parents can always imagine that they're not really his … and there is no greater or more heartening temptation than to try to find them, see what they look like,
and throw your love, or your hate, or both, in their faces.[8]
~ Emmanuel Carrère, French writer ~

21. Finding Me

During my second year as principal in Redwood City, the longing to find my birth parents continued to stir, and I began making inquiries with Iowa and Missouri state offices and local hospitals that might have my birth records. I wrote Tom Lazio again, mostly a repetition of my previous correspondence with him, and his responses mirrored the empathetic letters he'd sent me in the past. But in a brief comment at the end of one letter, Tom said he'd found a little more information that might be helpful. He enclosed two documents which, he said, were not part of my sealed record, so it was okay for him to share them with me.

They were a gold mine—what I had been looking for all these years! They finally gave me enough information to ratchet up my search. The first was a typewritten sheet dated two weeks after my birth, bearing the seal of the Willows Maternity Sanitarium in Kansas City. It showed the signature of my birth mother and the date. I knew in my heart this was signed at the moment I left her arms for good and she gave me up for adoption. Reading it, I let out long sigh.

The second document was written for the Division of Child Welfare of the State of Iowa:

> Mother's name: Gloria Jean Johnson. Age 22.
> Birthday: 1926. Hometown and address, date of high school graduation, 1944.
> Occupational history: Nurse.
> Mother's parents and siblings: names, address, education, and occupations.
> "Alleged" father: Wallace Alfred Russell. Age 34. Salesman for furniture company. Married.

Then came my original birth certificate:

> Name: Meredith Johnson [no middle name]
> Place of Birth: Jackson County, Kansas City, Missouri. Willows Maternity Sanitarium.
> Date of Birth: February 10, 1949
> Time of Birth: Not entered.
> Name of mother: Gloria Jean Johnson. White. Age 22.
> Other children: None.
> Signatures: Mother of Child, Medical Attendant (M.D.), Registrar.

I was now thirty-eight and dumbfounded by this new knowledge. I had yearned to know something about my identity—at least the names of my birth parents—since my teens. After years of aching to know more, the day had come. My mind was whirling. All I could do was sit in the quiet of my living room in Redwood City and feel the winds from the past blow through my heart and into the present. At last, I now knew my name and hers. In an instant, I understood this was not the end of my search, but the beginning. The hunt was on.

22. Finding Her

My name was Meredith Johnson. My mother was Gloria Jean Johnson. My father was Wallace Alfred Russell. Those three names ran through my mind in an unending loop, leaving me dizzy with excitement and, at the same time, short of breath. It didn't take long to conjure up a plan to find my birth mother. The plan had two parts.

In the summer of 1987, I flew back to Burlington, Iowa for my twenty-year class reunion. But my hidden agenda was to go to my birth mother's hometown to see if there was any evidence of her, such as a photo in a class yearbook or a listing in a phone directory. I took my mother's camper, telling her I would be visiting some old buddies who were on RAGBRAI, the Register's Annual Great Bicycle Ride Across Iowa. I had done RAGBRAI several times and had a lot of fun pedaling four hundred miles in ninety-degree heat across the state in a week, half-sloshed with cheap beer. I met up with my friends one night at a state park. We drank some beers and complained about the lack of decent food on the ride. But I said nothing about why I was actually there or where I was going. I left early the next morning and headed to a small town north of Des Moines without saying goodbye.

Iowa is notoriously hot and humid in late July, so I wore a breezy aloha shirt, short shorts, and flip flops—just like Tom Selleck. When I arrived, the high school was closed, and I realized I should have known—summer vacation, dummy!. My next and last resort was to go to the town's Carnegie-Evans Public Library. It was small, but had stolid, classic architecture and stood prominently in the town's center square. When I burst through the doors, all eyes turned toward me. Oh, I realized—Hawaiian shirt, flip flops. It must have looked as if I'd fallen out of the sky from another planet, or at minimum from the Castro in San Francisco, bringing back thoughts of entering the gas-station diner in mid-winter on my goofball drug deal. What a spectacle I must have been.

I walked directly to the head librarian and asked, "Do you have any high school yearbooks from around 1942 to 1945? I'm doing some family research and thought you might help me, because the high school is closed." With a trace of skepticism, she looked me up and down from my longish hair and mustache to my suntanned feet in rubbery lime-green-and-white sandals. Hoping to improve my chances, I shot her a sweet, demure smile.

She responded cordially but quizzically: "I'm not really sure. We don't keep those on the shelves anymore. Since those were the war years, I'm pretty sure yearbooks didn't have proper covers because of paper rationing. They just stapled them together. Let me see."

She turned to the wooden cabinet behind her and began rummaging through unorganized piles of newspapers and old journals. Then, with a loud "Aha!" she placed in front of me a worn and faded yearbook with a cardboard cover, dated 1942. This would have been Gloria Jean's sophomore year. I thanked her and found a small corner desk to peruse the yearbook. Everyone in the library was watching me intently and I could read their minds: *This guy's not from here! What's he up to?*

Voilà! Her name was in the index. I turned to the first page listed, and it was a class photo. I found her name in the caption: Gloria Jean Johnson, third row, second from the right. But the name and picture didn't look right to me. So, I went back to the index and then back to the page to make sure I hadn't made a mistake. I anticipated an attractive teenager, maybe cute, and the girl in the photo was neither. But as a friend warned me long ago, if I ever did find my birth mother, *maybe you won't find Elizabeth Taylor*. I admitted to myself that maybe I had idealized her in my mind, which might be blinding me to the truth of who she really was.

I went back to the index and turned to the pages of individual photos, and this time they matched my pre-conceived image of her. I saw a black and white photo of a very nice-looking girl who was about fifteen, and under the picture was her name: Gloria Jean Johnson. She was wearing a tight, light-colored sweater with a short necklace probably made of imitation pearls. Her lipstick was a little heavy, which may have been a bit risqué for rural Iowa in the 1940s. But her face! I saw a face that looked like mine at the same age. The same nose, mouth, and eyebrows as mine. Her dark eyes and dark hair were just like mine. Her hair was primped in stylish fashion. She might not have been Elizabeth Taylor, but she actually resembled a young Gene Tierney, the femme fatale of 1940s movies. I had hit the jackpot. This girl, this sweet good-looking girl from an obscure town in the heart of Iowa was my mother! Her photograph took my breath away.

I stared out the large bay window as tears welled-up and dripped onto my shorts. I gazed at townspeople on the sidewalk outside, fanning themselves with whatever they could find to stay cool. Not a soul among them knew what I had just found. I could hardly believe it myself. Before standing to leave, I gently stroked the yearbook cover, and tried to imagine Gloria Jean back then, and all that must have happened to her before she gave birth to me. By stroking the yearbook, I didn't know if I was comforting her or myself. The image of us together, as mother and child, felt alive—not something from the past—but here and now in her hometown forty years later. On my way out, I realized I might need addresses for Gloria's parents and other relatives. I spotted a phone book, and when no one was looking, I took it.

For reasons I still can't explain to myself, I did not take advantage of being in a town where almost anyone would know a Johnson. And I did not try to locate the street that was listed for her parents in the Willows' document. I felt timid about even driving by that address. Regardless, I knew I could now find her in person. Like Babe Ruth pointing to centerfield, I knew the ball was going to be a home run before I hit it. I knew I would find her, alive or dead.

I got to work on part two of my plan when I returned to Redwood City. I crafted a letter to every Johnson in the county that sounded legitimate but did not give away what I was up to:

> I am looking for an old acquaintance for the purpose of a reunion. Her name is Gloria Jean Johnson. She is a graduate of the [name withheld] high school and worked for a time as a nurse in Iowa City around 1948. She is approximately sixty years old. Please send me whatever you believe to be her forwarding address.

I then signed it: Dr. S. R. Rowley, hoping her relatives would think that our "reunion" might be related to our mutual doctor/nurse history and enclosed a stamped envelope hoping this would expedite a response. Three weeks later, I received an envelope the size of a small thank-you card addressed to Dr. S. R. Rowley, with no return address. Inside the envelope was a small piece of paper folded neatly in half that read, simply: "I think this might help you." Below it was a printed address with the name Gloria Jean Wilkes attached to it. I guess this meant she was married, or had been married.

I was afraid that if I contacted her by letter, it might expose a past that no one knew about. But after three weeks, I decided to take a chance, and I wrote introducing myself and asking if I might visit her:

> Dear Gloria,
>
> How else can I begin but to say that I am the boy you gave birth to on February 10, 1949. Wanting to meet you has been the long-standing desire of my life. Back in your hometown, I

found your picture in your class yearbook from 1942. You and I were practically twins when we were each that age. Finding your picture sent a chill down my spine.

I want you to know that when we do meet one day, I have no other wish or agenda than seeing you face-to-face. Other than hearing your voice, seeing you in the flesh, and sharing what we can of our past lives, there is nothing else I want from you.

My greatest fear in looking for you is that you will say NO to meeting me. I have already accepted that possibility, knowing that my presence in your life may cause you or others great pain. But somehow, I want to believe that you want to see me as much as I want to see you.

I think you should know that I have had a very good life. My adopted parents were great for me. I've gotten a B.A. in college and went on to get a Ph.D. in education at Stanford University in 1984. I had one long-range girlfriend when I lived in Seattle, and I now live with a teacher who works in my school. But to date, I have not been married and I have no children.

I hope you will write back to me soon. I just need to know you have read this letter. I just need to know.

Oh, yes! "Meredith" never made it through the adoption process. I am Stephen Robert Rowley. If you can get used to it, "Steve" will be just fine.

With my love,

[signed Steve]

After I wrote my letter, I left it on my desk just to sit. I was too nervous—too unsure about myself and what I was doing. I was definitely unsure about her. Who was she? What had happened to her since 1949? A week later, I impulsively grabbed the letter, stuffed it in an envelope, and left it for the mailman. A week after that, there was a message on my phone answering machine:

> Hi, Steve. This is Patricia Jacobs. People call me Patty. My married name is Jacobs but my maiden name is Wilkes. My mother is Gloria Jean Wilkes, but she goes by Jean. Her maiden's name was Johnson. My sister Charlotte and I intercepted your letter to Mom. Charlotte is just a year younger than you. We weren't sure she should see your letter, as she is under the care of a psychiatrist. We need his approval first. Please call me, it's a long story. Bye.

How I learned more of the story about Jean is fuzzy in my memory. Between letters and phone calls, I found out that Jean and her ex-husband had been divorced for many years. Following the divorce, Jean needed to work to support Patty, Charlotte, and their younger brother. But she had trouble holding down a job. She had bounced in and out of nursing positions for abusing and stealing pharmaceuticals from the hospitals where she worked. Her addiction to drugs and alcohol increased over the years. Eventually her license as a registered nurse was revoked. As young women in their twenties, Charlotte and Patty eventually moved from the Midwest to the Green Mountains of Vermont, living off the grid. Charlotte had been married, divorced, remarried, and now had four children between the two men. Grandmother Jean joined them for a while, but eventually she moved on to Boston.

Living alone and on welfare, her drug addiction and alcoholism led to early stages of dementia.

Only eight weeks before I sent my letter, Jean had been found wandering the streets, pushing a grocery cart, and acting irrationally. Either the police or her welfare caseworker contacted the girls to let them know that Jean was in a locked facility for mandatory rehabilitation. She was later placed in a halfway house and remained under the care of a psychiatrist. According to Patty, she was doing better and had just been assigned to state-sponsored housing, where she shared a small apartment with a woman who was struggling with a major mental disorder.

I understood Patty's hesitancy, but I was undeterred. I assured her I would not physically approach Jean without the approval of the psychiatrist and her. That said, I knew I was going one way or the other. I simply had to see my mother's face, even from across the street. I was mightily relieved when Patty gave her tentative approval for me to visit her, but said she needed an okay from Charlotte. I went ahead anyway and made reservations to fly to Boston right after Christmas and back to San Francisco on New Year's Day 1988.

Later that fall, I received a long letter from Charlotte. This letter, and many she sent later, made me feel less anxious about wanting to meet our mother in person. Her letters also made me feel a deep kinship with her. She too had a BA in English, and she later had worked as a newspaper reporter. Her warm and direct way was reassuring, but some of her words made me really sad.

Dear Steve,

You know nothing of me, yet I have known you as my lost brother. I have always been in hope of finding you. Patty tells me you are doing well. I'm so happy to hear that.

I, unfortunately, look upon my childhood as a dismal affair. Our whole family lacked love. Mom was loving but she married Dad on the rebound from your birth father. This turned out to be a fatal mistake. She is now a very insecure person with low self-esteem and had drawn down upon herself a tragedy much like a Shakespearean character. Despite her intelligence and many talents, she sees herself as a "dummy" and a victim.

Dad had a hard time keeping a job so Mom had to go to work when we were young. Dad would get violent with me, and when Mom took me to the hospital, she would make up stories about how I got hurt from an accident. She was pregnant with me before they were married. Dad's problems got worse over time, so they divorced when I was 17. She was a wreck. He left glib, cold-hearted as always. It is a blessing that I found religion, which has helped me cope and have faith. God forgive me if I have laid it on too thick and added to your burden.

Please know that the news of you has allowed tremendous happiness to enter my heart. I hope you know now that you were spared, you were the lucky one.

My love, too.
[signed, Charlotte Wilkes Babcock]

For as lucky as I was to discover the truth, the stories from Patty and Charlotte were tender but worrisome. There was such a disconnection in my mind between the youth and charm of Jean's yearbook photo and the picture they painted of her now—disabled and broken later in life. It was all so tragically sad. I would never fully appreciate the trauma that Jean's other three children suffered from divorce, domestic abuse, and physical and emotional abandonment. I could only imagine the wounds they carried into their adult lives. Yet, I remained determined to see Jean, even though I was increasingly uncertain of who or what I might find—not Elizabeth Taylor, that was for sure.

23. Mother and Child Reunion

The day to meet my biological mother had arrived at last. It was cold and overcast in Boston on December 29, 1987. I stayed at a large hotel downtown, although my scheduled rendezvous was near Roxbury. As per our plan, Patty came to my hotel room at 11 a.m. so we could get to know each other a little before going to see our mother. Patty had moved years earlier to Quincy, Massachusetts to be closer to Jean because of her declining health.

When Patty called my room from the lobby, we both sounded jittery. After all, what *do* you say to your half-brother or half-sister who is otherwise a complete stranger? Once she entered my room, we laughed in unison because we didn't look or sound like each other at all. She had sandy colored hair and was much shorter than me. The first thing she said was, "My God, you look just like Mom, more than any of us do!"

That was a surprise. Then we shared stories of our respective lives and our families, and Patty reiterated what Charlotte had told me. She and her siblings had always known about me. My arrival into their lives was not a question of *if*, but *when*. Patty tried to prepare me for meeting Jean. Her ground floor apartment was in a large apartment building in a rather sketchy part of town. She wasn't sure if Jean's roommate would be there. And yes, Jean knew of my plan to take us to a late lunch, an idea I thought might help break the ice. But Patty seemed unsure.

"I can't tell with Mom anymore. I have to be honest; I don't know how this will go." Hearing this my anxiety shifted into high gear, and I tried to assure both of us that things would work out. I had ordered flowers to give her, so maybe that would help smooth things a bit.

With that, Patty led me to her car to drive us to Jean's place. I felt nauseous and claustrophobic in her cramped Honda Civic. We passed several miles of unremarkable stone tenement buildings and abandoned brick factories until we turned a corner and parked outside a nondescript apartment building that looked like the others around it, certainly not Elizabeth Taylor's place.

As Patty and I approached the ground-level door of Jean's apartment, I reminded myself to breathe. I forced myself to inhale the crisp December air, as though breathing itself was an unnatural act. After Patty's three forceful knocks, Jean appeared through a small crack in the door. I could tell she was hesitating. When she finally opened the door more widely, she stationed herself near the wall of the narrow foyer. She appeared to be wearing a short brown-colored wig, which didn't compliment her appearance. She was shorter than I had imagined. She pivoted and stood sideways to the door and me, which revealed a heavy stoop in her shoulders. She wore oversized, dark-rimmed glasses long out of fashion. But beyond my quick assessment, I didn't have a moment to consider what her appearance told me about her. A lot of women her age looked similar. Patty announced my arrival in a measured and courtly way.

"Mom, this is Steve. He's finally here from California." Then I heard words that I was not remotely prepared for.

"Who the hell gave you my phone number and address? I didn't ask you to come. What gives you the right?!"

Patty became unglued before my mind could register what I had just heard. She gasped, "Mom, what are you saying? How could you?! Stop it and let us in!"

As though nudged by an invisible hand, I took a half-step toward her and spoke with a gentle and measured tone. "Hello, Jean. I just wanted to introduce myself to you. It wasn't that somebody just gave me your address. Let's just say it took me some time to find you." Then I extended a box of long-stemmed white roses to her. "Here, these are for you."

After a very long pause, I heard her say with more resignation and a slight edge of resentment, "Well, no one has ever given me flowers."

Her words pierced my heart. But she adjusted without a fuss and ushered us into the kitchen, where she offered Patty and me each a padded plastic chair, and she sat in another across the gray Formica table. The kitchen, 1950s in style, was spotless, but felt and looked dreary. The gray plastic countertop matched the table. Faded wood-veneer cabinets framed an old-fashioned white ceramic sink, rusted around the drain. The sink and countertop looked as if they hadn't been used for some time. Once seated, and when I could collect my wits, I was struck by how much Jean and I looked alike, even though I was much taller and twenty years younger.

I nervously looked around and spotted a small living room furnished with a sagging three-piece sectional couch, an old Philco TV with rabbit ears, and a stuffed brown Naugahyde easy chair with a crooked floor lamp next to it.

Sensing my interest, she announced, "You know, they have some of my personal stuff in storage still. Mostly my books."

"Oh, really. How many do you have?" I half-heartedly replied, to be polite.

"Oh, I don't know, more than five hundred."

Before that moment, I didn't think my attention could have been on any higher alert. But when she mentioned five hundred books, sirens began to howl in my head. While I was trying to compute what it meant, I noticed the two framed posters from the Museum of Fine Arts on the wall.

"So, I see you like the Museum of Fine Arts," I queried. "I like those posters."

Jean pointed to the poster hanging beneath a cheap circular clock on the wall behind Patty.

"Oh, yeah," she said nonchalantly with a nod, gesturing to the poster labelled *Circles in a Circle,* 1923. "Kandinsky has always been one of my favorites of the moderns, but I actually prefer his earlier work in Russia. You gotta like that one there, though. He was one of the first to deal with stuff that comes up from the unconscious. Very spiritual. By the time he moved to Paris in the Thirties, he was really ahead of his time."

I thought back to what Patty told me earlier. Jean's drug and alcohol abuse had been so severe that she had wandered the streets and gone missing for days before they found her. Now she was giving me a lesson in modern European art history. I simply couldn't believe what my senses told me was true.

As if on cue, my brown eyes fell on hers, and for a moment, everything around us stopped. I took a deep, audible breath and exhaled slowly. I said, "I see," which was one of great understatements I ever uttered.

Our conversation soon moved to politics and to the defining moment of the day. Jean launched into a detailed analysis of the records of the Democratic hopefuls who would likely run against the odds-on favorite for President, Ronald Reagan, in the fall election. She clearly despised Reagan and everything he stood for. Although I am not much of a joke-teller, I told a joke about Reagan that was quite funny. But in that moment, it was stupendously hilarious, as Jean burst out in a roar at the punch line. Her laugh was warm, smart, and deep from her belly.

We had shared more than a clever political joke. Her soul opened to mine in that moment. I could hear myself in her laugh, and I could see myself in her eyes. I could sense her mind working, just as mine did. I could feel the unmistakable embrace of our souls as our guardian angels wrapped their wings about our shoulders and pulled us together, but not just in this moment. The twenty-two-year-old young woman from Iowa and her infant son who were separated long ago were now reunited, if only for a fleeting moment. I had found my mother, and she had found her boy, at last.

As if I needed a drop more from her, I hesitantly queried a few minutes later, in a very roundabout way. Had she thought about me much, or thought of me at all, on my birthday? She held my question like a sacred talisman in her palm and I could sense her reverie. Every birthday of mine had been a lonesome ritual that only one other person on earth could appreciate. It was a question I needed not ask. I watched her tears well up. And with the most tender voice, she responded with self-assured clarity.

"Yes, of course. I always think of you on February 10, and a lot of other days too. I know you have a mother, a really good mother and father. Look at you—so handsome and so successful, what with Stanford and all. But you are my son too. I never, ever forget that."

This was the one thing I wanted to hear from her. I responded in kind with my tears and I placed my hand on top of hers. Nothing more need be said. I spent the rest of the long afternoon with Jean until we were worn out. We never thought about lunch.

As planned, I paid a visit the next day to my half-sister Charlotte, who lived in the hills outside Milford, Massachusetts. That's a story in itself—full of grandkids, chronic health issues, financial challenges, and a devout but eclectic religious philosophy. Charlotte had prepared a small box of photographs of her mother for me. It contained her high school graduation picture, a recent picture with several of her grandchildren, and picture of Jean in her nursing uniform and cap from years ago.

There was another photo, which I had framed and keep on my office bookshelf at home. Jean is dressed in an olive-green, military-style jacket with red epaulets and a white silk blouse. She is wearing a jaunty-looking beret with a large military-looking pin on it. This might have been evidence of her being in the Iowa Women's Auxiliary Army Corps, after she graduated high school in 1944. I can't be sure. Gloria Jean Johnson looks radiant and full of life. Her easy smile is cheerful and innocent. She looks so happy.

I sometimes refuse to think how life would change so dramatically for her a few years later. When I think of her, this is the image I default to—not a weary and confused woman pushing a shopping cart, living in a downtrodden apartment building. Charlotte and I stayed up the entire night, drinking tea, holding hands, and wondering if we knew each other in a previous life. Such is the stuff of dreams.

After leaving Charlotte's home and her family in the hills near Milford, I returned to Jean's apartment the next day to say goodbye. When I arrived, she introduced me to her pleasant female roommate, who was being treated for schizophrenia.

"Millie, this is Steve, my son. He came all the way from California to see me—mostly to see my Kandinsky, she laughed. I just wanted you to meet him before he flies back tomorrow morning. You know, us Iowa folks are a punctual lot. I have to make sure he gets some sleep before his plane leaves in the morning." Then she chuckled again.

Later that evening we hugged as I stood to leave, but I can't remember much after that. I do recall that we held each other closely for a very long time. We both knew that we might not see each other again. Before I opened the front door, I brushed a few strands of her wig back and gently caressed and kissed her forehead with total, loving deliberation. And then I was gone. Out the door. I kept my head down as I walked into the freezing evening air in a neighborhood that I knew I would never visit again.

The next morning, I sat alone in a back row of a mostly empty Boeing 737 bound for San Francisco. I hadn't slept much and I was completely drained. The loud engines brought the jet to takeoff speed. The fuselage then lifted at a sharp angle and headed to the western horizon. The whole thing—the search and the reunion with Jean—spun in my head, clenched my heart, and twisted around my throat. I could scarcely breathe.

When the jet leveled at 35,000 feet, I thought of all the time I had spent and all the obstacles I had encountered in my search for her. I had actually done it. I had completed my quest. I had found my birth mother and discovered the ineffable bond between us. I tried to imagine what it must have been like for the two of us, the last time we parted from each other almost forty years earlier. I was a ten-day-old infant, and she was a twenty-two-year-old woman about to give up her only child.

Her sacrifice was heart-wrenching in a way that only the two of us could know. Each of us carried the painful, implicit memory of our separation. What I learned from our reunion was that her wound profoundly changed her life for the worse. As for my wound, one day far in the future, I would see it as a gift, wrapped in a package of longing and incompleteness. Without my wound, my fate would have reversed itself. And surely, I would not be writing this memoir. Without my wound, the touchstone of my humanity, I would never have become the man I was meant to be.

With a torrent of feelings, memories, and imagined events stirring so deeply within me, I could feel a crack in my heart opening faster than I could hold it back. I dashed to an aft lavatory and sat on a small toilet seat lid alongside an equally small sink. I began to shake … and then I broke open, like a dam overwhelmed by a deluge of decades of stored rain water. The flood overwhelmed me, sucked me under, and would not relent until I struggled to the surface for air. After what seemed a lifetime, I returned to my seat, where I leaned back, closed my eyes, and fell into a restless slumber, from which my dreams failed to report.

PART SIX

The journey of the orphan is to become in touch with
all that he or she can be. To become in touch with the
creativity that exists within us all to become whole.
This, combined with self-reflection, reestablishes hope
and a sense that I have a future.[9]
~ Audrey Punnett, Jungian analyst and writer ~

24. New Directions

When I returned to the Bay Area, I realized I had taken few notes
or photos when I was with Jean and my half-sisters. I panicked
when I couldn't remember the wealth of background information
I'd been given about her and about my birth.

At the beginning of our conversation, she had said, "You
probably want me to tell you about your father. Well, I don't
really remember much of anything." And she then went on to talk
about him for an hour. Once home, I couldn't remember anything
she'd said about him. Kandinsky, I could remember. But my birth
father? No.

The refrain "How fucking stupid can you be?" banged in
my brain like wooden sticks on a tin drum for weeks. I was now
back to scratch in knowing anything about my birth father. His
paper trail was nonexistent and my interest in locating him had
faded. From the beginning, my search was for my mother, not
him. Jean was what I felt had been missing in me. Likely it was
Jean I was looking for in the women I had pursued over the years.

I was proud that I had fulfilled my promise to find her, and that our reunion entirely surpassed what I thought might be possible. Despite forgetting many of the details she shared with me, I was at peace about my adoption and her. To quote Walt Whitman, "We were together, I forget the rest."

I put my adoption records and correspondence into a metal file box, and twenty more years would pass until I needed to revisit its contents. Three years after our reunion in Massachusetts, Charlotte called to tell me Jean had died, sharing little detail. There was no emotion in her words.

Maybe her death was a relief to her other children too. I don't recall if there was a service for her; in any case I was not invited. I felt more alone than sad that evening, recounting what it was in me I had found in her. Regardless of the details, my memory of Jean is visceral, and it remains alive today.

Back in the Bay Area, no sooner did I embrace my work and my budding relationship with Johanna than I felt the itch of professional ambition once again, and this time I was armed with an arsenal of leadership skills and experience.

After my tenure in Redwood City, I would change jobs or occupations every three to five years, a pattern not uncommon among those climbing a career ladder. But at the time my rapid moves from place to place made me wonder if I was just a wanderer, or if I would ever find the right groove, the purpose of my life. I felt like Carlos Castaneda in *The Teachings of Don Juan*, wracked by uncertainty about finding his seat on the dirt floor of a small adobe hut.

I kind of knew who I was, but I couldn't find my place. I didn't know where I wanted to go or what I wanted to do next. I was full of ambition about making schools and school districts work well, but I was looking outside myself for clues. Enmeshed in a false narrative of my presumed heroic destiny, I didn't have the presence of mind to ask my soul what it wanted of me. Had I been more self-aware, I might have recognized that I confused outer-world challenges with the call of my soul. Fortunately, fate had its way of turning my life inside out whenever I needed it, keeping me off-balance, as I struggled to find myself through my profession. As I eventually realized, the most important clues were within my heart, not my work.

Just as my career was gaining momentum, the field of public education underwent a series of seismic events in policy and politics that changed the terrain of teaching and learning. Presidents, governors, Congress, state legislatures, and even the Bill and Melinda Gates Foundation launched wave after wave of poorly thought-out policies and initiatives, starting with the publication of *A Nation at Risk,* a landmark report of the US National Commission on Excellence in Education, in 1983. The well-meaning but flawed reforms targeted important outcomes but sadly lacked effective implementation strategies. What followed in the coming decades included No Child Left Behind, "high stakes" standardized testing, Outcome-Based Education, college readiness for all, high school exit exams, school report cards, Pre-K readiness programs, whole language, the replacement of vocationally-focused classes such as auto mechanics with Science Technology Engineering Math (STEM) coursework, and pre-programmed laptop computers for all. I'm painting this picture in black and white, which of course is not entirely fair or accurate. Schools did need more accountability and students could benefit from having higher standards. My peeve was that these policies made schools into outcome factories, the very model progressive educators were trying to break. Moreover, they were crafted from the top down and thus they struggled to get buy-in where it was needed the most: from the grass roots.

More importantly, very little of all this helped close the achievement gap or make US students more competitive with other countries. Arguably, these policies made things worse; and in the process, they made teaching into a didactic exercise that turned kids off. These policies took the fun out of teaching and learning. To me, that was the crime. It's no wonder I felt so at odds with my profession through most of my career. If I had known this policy morass would be the backdrop of my professional future, I might have quit. But I didn't. What I did know is that it was time to move on to a position of higher authority and greater challenge.

While I was trying to decide my next career move, fate upended me. Shock of shocks, Johanna and I decided to get married. At the age of forty, I actually felt ready to marry and settle down. But I wasn't tying the knot just to settle down. I had found a partner for life. We shared many interests and tastes in sports, travel, movies, food, wine, and a stable homelife. The impact of this earth-shattering news on my friends was huge, like the episode of *Seinfeld* when Jerry tells Elaine that George Costanza is getting married. Elaine explodes with a super loud, "Get Out!" and pushes Jerry so hard that he falls backwards into the next room. It was that big. Steve Rowley is getting married—*Get Out!*

25. Simple Twists of Fate

I left my job in Redwood City in June 1990, and Johanna and I were married in December in Saratoga, California. Getting married was the good news, but taking a job as a faculty member at the University of Idaho-Moscow was one of the dumbest things I've done, though not as dumb as the drug deal in the blizzard! I simply didn't belong there. Nor was I enamoured with attending school administrator meetings in a backwoods hunting lodge in the Idaho Panhandle and in a Couer d'Alene bowling alley. This job and the faculty position I took a year later at Washington State University, however, turned out to be indispensable steps for Johanna and me in fulfilling our mutual destinies, which turned out to be not in education. It was a stroke of fate that someone arrived in our lives we could never have anticipated.

My Stanford education and having been principal of a progressive school were of little help in my new positions. Although the people at both universities, and in the Pullman School District, where Johanna taught elementary school in Washington State a few miles west of Moscow, Idaho, were certainly nice enough. Indeed, some of those relationships endure today. But I was a fish out of water in small-town, rural university settings. Though raised in Iowa, at that point in my life I must have reeked of California, and the clock seemed set back a decade or more in the Inland Empire of the Pacific Northwest. I often wondered aloud, *What are we doing here? What was I thinking when I accepted these positions?* I had no way of knowing it was all part of what later seemed like a preordained plan.

At an educational conference in Seattle, I met a veteran superintendent from a school district on the west side of the Cascades, a region Johanna and I kiddingly referred to as civilization. He was doing some innovative things in his district, so I thought he might understand my plight. I mentioned that I was restless—eager to get back into action as a central office administrator, and to be in a progressive system where I could apply what had learned in California.

He told me, "There's a new superintendent in Bellingham. He just moved here from California. I think he's still got a position open, something to do with school improvement. Check it out."

I did check and eventually got the job. When we moved to Bellingham, Washington Johanna got a job teaching gifted students in nearby Ferndale, and I was the new Assistant Superintendent of K-12 Schools and School Improvement in the Bellingham School District. I supervised eighteen principals and their schools, and was given the longer-range task of creating a system of school site councils. On top of that, I was involved in innovative design processes for two high schools and one new middle school. I was a busy, happy boy.

Six months later, as I returned home from a Sunday afternoon lunch with a friend, Johanna met me at the door with a distressed look on her face. "I don't know what you should hear first? The Superintendent had a massive heart attack and is being medevacked to Everett for open heart surgery. They don't know if he's going to make it. You are supposed to call the School Board President right now. The Board had an emergency session and appointed you Acting Superintendent, starting tomorrow."

Beyond my shock, I understood I had been temporarily promoted over the two other assistant superintendents—both of whom were much more experienced and established than me. Wow! I always wanted to be a superintendent, but not this way. I was in a daze all night, and had to clear my head for the next day.

I would open our regular Monday morning Leadership Team meeting with the Board President at my side—a sure indication that I had the full support of the Board. The team, like me, was in shock about the Superintendent and in shock that the Board had asked me to lead things. And lead I did, that morning and for the next six weeks until he returned. I felt great support from all but one of my teammates, as everyone knew this was an emergency situation and I was on the spot.

One of my assistant superintendent colleagues was jealous that I'd been named, as he had seniority over me by a mile. What he didn't know, or chose not to know, was that the Superintendent thought he was a bit of sycophant. I saw him as a consummate bureaucrat, which was not endearing to others or me. But the Superintendent showed me, by example, how to work with difficult people—people who, by their very natures, will never be team players. I had to learn what was right about Mr. Bureaucrat. As Jim March might have said, any jackass can tell you what's wrong with him—tell me what is right about him.

Johanna and I were fully engaged in our respective jobs, doing what we loved and did best. With the little time we shared when we weren't working, we made weekend jaunts to Vancouver

BC, Seattle, and the Oregon Coast. We were a childless couple, happy and determined to keep it that way. As we often told ourselves and others: "We gave at the office." Our professional lives were full to the brim with kids. We would occasionally gloat that we were lucky be able to go out to dinner when we wanted and that we didn't have dirty diapers to deal with. And we could sleep in on weekends. We both loved kids, and at the same time, we were fine that we didn't have to take them home with us.

Just before Halloween in 1993, Johanna came home late after a full day of teacher-parent conferences, and shared a bit about her day. Then she said, in an off-handed manner, "I heard something terrible today. Remember Alexa, the mother of one of my kids? I had her other daughter last year. Alexa had this cute little boy with her at open house. The boy's mother was just killed in a horrible car crash. Alexa's taking care of him now, but I think she wants to have the boy adopted. Here's his picture."

She tossed a small Polaroid photo onto the coffee table in front of the TV, and I glanced at it, then set it aside. I growled a kind of *humph* under my breath in response to what I imagined she might be thinking. But I knew there was no way we would be ever be interested in adopting a child—a four-year-old in this case. The boy was a cutie all right. Dark hair with dark eyes, a roundish face, smooth skin, and a sliver of smile that could melt hearts. But what caught my attention was that, in the photo, he was straddling the large arm of an old stuffed couch like he was riding a horse. It looked nearly identical to a picture taken of me at that same age in Burlington. I had a sense of déjà vu every time I looked at his picture, but I said nothing. That photo stayed on the coffee table for three weeks, and we never spoke about it. Every time we watched TV, the picture just sat there, like he was watching me.

After three weeks, I came home from work one afternoon, picked up the photo, and asked Johanna, "So, when are we going to meet this little boy?" And that was that. Galaxies would soon collide and our three lives would never be the same.

26. Finding the Boy

The plot line of the unfolding drama was becoming clear, and we sensed that our timing had been impeccable since leaving Redwood City. We needed to live and work in Bellingham and have all the stars line up so that Johanna would be at the teacher-parent conference just after the boy came into Alexa's life. I needed to be reluctant to see him at first, to allow him to adjust to his mother's disappearance, and for him to figure out that Alexa was not the person he wanted to be with. Johanna needed the uncanny luck to have Alexa's daughters in her classroom and have a relationship with Alexa before the boy came on the scene. Then there was the photo of him looking a lot like me at four years old. And no small piece of the puzzle was me coming to terms with being adopted myself. Looking back, all these elements needed to line up like dominoes so we could find our boy.

Little Eddie Winfield was due at our house on Halloween morning, which that year was a Saturday. We were out of our minds with nervous energy and curiosity. We had a long list of things we wanted to do with him. *But would he like them? What if we ran out of things to do? Would he like us? And what would he like to eat? Could he go to the bathroom by himself? Oh, lord! Did I say we were nervous?*

We saw Alexa and Eddie through the glass panel as they approached the front door. I don't recall whether she was holding his hand. When we opened the door to greet them, Johanna and I both got on our knees to be at eye level with him. We said our names and shook his soft, tiny hand. He was totally adorable. His clothes were clean but shabby and ill-fitting, as though everything he wore came from Goodwill. We looked past all that and just saw *him*. We repeated our promise to have him ready to go home by 5:00 p.m. and quickly said goodbye to Alexa.

As soon as she was gone, his face lit up—not with just a big smile, but with a sigh of relief and wonder. We each took one of his hands and ushered him into the kitchen, which like the rest of the house, had a very modern look to it. Everything was spotless, yet comfortable. His eyes got bigger as we showed him the view of Lake Whatcom from our deck. Then we led him to where we slept and let him wander through our two other bedrooms and the all-important second bathroom. *Do you have to go? Just let us know.* We knew this would be a special day. And we could tell from his clothes and haircut alone how difficult his life had been. We wondered how well he ate and if he'd recently been to a doctor. We could see how different his life was from ours and our own childhoods.

Eddie and I played in the front yard with a nerf football and we hit whiffle golf balls with a shortened putter. It was obvious that Eddie had never thrown a football or hit a golf ball. Later, Johanna set him on her lap and read a pile of books to him. He was transfixed. We fed him a grilled cheese sandwich with small carrot strips and dip for lunch. The kid was famished! He gobbled the sandwich, but was reluctant to ask for more. We could see he was too shy to ask for anything more than he was given. Then we set up a Halloween cookie assembly line. *Yes! You can paint the face of the big pumpkin cookie orange, white, or black. Yes, you can squiggle-decorate his face with green or black frosting that comes from a tube that looks like tooth paste. You can make him look silly, or scary, or like me—Steve! And yes, yes. Of course, yes. You can eat some now and you can take the others home with you to share with Alexa's daughters. Sure, you can!*

Our spirits soared. We were having so much fun with him that we didn't dare stop and acknowledge the painful evidence that, at the very least, he had been mistreated, most likely through neglect. We learned later that it was much worse. It pained us to find out just how desperate his circumstances were, living with his single mother in a low-rent apartment, with a man or two intermittently serving as her boyfriend. But it wouldn't have changed a thing for us if we had known about his troubled past.

He seemed to revel in every activity. We could tell his school-readiness skills were sub-par, but he was a very bright boy. Within just a few hours, he opened to our laps and our hugs with such tenderness of spirit. What a joy to know that he liked us as much as we liked him. Nothing got in his way to connect with us right off the bat. It was a marvel to behold him and a blessing for us to share this time with him.

By 4:30 it was getting dark, and the doorbell rang. As Johanna led Alexa into the entryway, not the house, she called with a high-pitched faux cheerfulness. "Eddie! Aunt Alexa is here. I'm sorry but it's time to go." Without hesitation, Eddie leapt to his feet, leaned toward me with his hand covering the side of his mouth, and whispered in my ear words that I will never forget. "I don't like Aunt Alexa."

My heart broke for him. His mother had been killed only a few weeks before, although you would never know it from him, as he seemed so happy to be with us. Now, he was living with a woman he didn't like. This boy was an orphan. I knew something about that. I knew a lot about him, regardless of the details of his past. From the heart of my soul to his, I knew something of his inner desolation and hurt, which did not appear on the surface. Johanna and I knew something else. A gift like this beautiful boy comes your way maybe once in a lifetime, so don't blow it! I'm not a believer in any faith, but a God by any name led us to Eddie on Halloween Day 1993. Or did Eddie find his way to us?

Once Alexa was out the door with Eddie, I proclaimed the obvious: "We've got to adopt that boy!" I did not need to hear Johanna's response, as we held each other, and together we made another proclamation. "He's our boy now. We will do whatever's needed to raise him as our son. The adoption process, however difficult it may be, is simply a trial we'll endure. We'll do everything in our power to keep him."

We had found the perfect child for us, even though we thought we weren't looking for one. He had appeared in our lives like magic, as though it was meant to be. Here we were: one moment a couple ardently reluctant to become parents, and the next, a couple who would pursue his adoption with unwavering commitment. From that moment forward, we were utterly determined. As for me, it was my time to pay forward the great luck I had with my own adoption. This wasn't an obligation—it was my honor.

During one of Eddie's many visits to our house during the adoption process, out of nowhere, he grabbed our coat sleeves and said with such sweet sincerity. "Steeeve? Joaaana? Would you bedopt me?" Without another word, we threw our arms around his small body, tears streaming down our cheeks.

"Of course, we will we adopt you, Eddie honey! From this moment on, we are a family. You can't stay with us until the judge says it's okay, but even so, we are a real family now!"

In the weeks to come, there were a flurry of questionnaires to fill out, lawyers to consult, home visits from social workers, and a great deal of angst when we learned that five other couples wanted to adopt him too. This was a trial in itself. Three of those couples already knew Eddie and his mother. Then, we "flunked" our first home visit, after being sequestered in separate rooms and questioned individually by the social worker. We never figured out why we needed another home visit by a new social worker after her interrogation, but we covered our bets by joining the most liberal Presbyterian Church in Bellingham. As you might guess, this was tough for me to swallow, especially when the minister exhorted his enthusiastic congregants to lift and sway their arms above their heads and proclaim that Jesus was in our midst with a mighty *hallelujah!* If this was the liberal church, I couldn't fathom what the more conventional Presbyterian Church was like,

Eddie's birth father (who was living in Northern Africa at the time), through his attorney, sent pages of questions for us to answer, including queries about our politics and religious beliefs. He then also said *no* to our request to take Eddie on an out-of-town trip at Christmas—all of which threw us into a panic. We lived on pins and needles for what seemed a lifetime.

Eddie's birth parents were Canadian and European. His father, the Canadian, was married to someone else and had several grown children. A college graduate, he had a successful career. While on temporary assignment in Europe, he had an affair with a young woman barely out of high school. After that, he was reassigned somewhere else, and the young woman, now pregnant, followed him. After she gave birth to Eddie, his birth father was unwilling to play any role in the boy's life, and his mother took him to be with relatives in the Pacific Northwest.

Eddie's mother made several attempts to marry men who could support them financially, which would allow her to apply for a Green Card. She would leave Eddie alone for hours in their small apartment, in the van of one of her boyfriends at his work site, at state-sponsored daycare programs, or at the Lighthouse Mission Ministries in Bellingham. Other times she would dress him up in an old-fashioned bow tie and wool vest, and take him with her to ask friends for money simply to get by.

On the day of her accident, without saying goodbye to him, she drove toward the SeaTac International Airport to turn herself in to US immigration authorities. She was being deported and would soon be returned to her country of origin. On the way, her car sped into the back of a semi-trailer truck on Interstate 5, and she died immediately. Eddie's father, still overseas, still wanted no part in caring for him, save paying for an attorney to handle his adoption. To my knowledge, Eddie never grieved her untimely death. Most likely, a part of him just shut down. But miraculously, he remained a loving and vibrant child, ready for a new life. I knew that feeling as well.

As Johanna was talking to Eddie about becoming a family, out-of-the blue he said, "Mom, I think we've been looking for each other for a long time." He didn't mean we were looking for each other in the past few months. His meaning was unmistakable.

He meant we were in search before any of us knew one another—maybe through past lives or by the hand of fate. Who knows?

Surely this was true of me in a slightly different way. I cannot say for a fact that I was in search of a child, unconsciously, who would be the "something" I felt was missing inside me. Looking back, that might have been true. But it was more than that. For me, finding the boy meant finding the wounded boy, the orphan inside Eddie—like finding a miner trapped in a collapsed mineshaft. I would not leave that lost boy behind. For both Johanna and me, finding Eddie and providing him with the life he deserved—the life he was meant to live—was a timeless moment brimming with grace and redemption. This was the gift we embraced with total gratitude. I am happy to say we did not blow it.

Finding the boy. From the moment I laid eyes on Eddie, and when he told me he didn't like Aunt Alexa, I could see the lost boy inside him. It was then I rediscovered the orphan in me.

In the course of a few short months, as we formed an indelible bond as a family, each of our lives were transformed. Johanna and I had never shared such happiness, and I think it was also true for Eddie at that time. Despite the many ups and downs of my career and our lives that were yet to come, no event, no reunion, and no spiritual awakening could match the utter joy of our adoption of Edward Stephen Rowley.

27. A Vision Come True

Suddenly, as if out of the blue, I was a father. Yet, I found myself once again eager to move to a new place, somewhere I could put my knowledge and experience into action. I wanted to do what I had done in Seattle and Redwood City, but at a larger scale—to create a new school model as the centerpiece of an innovative vision for a school district. Few school boards look for superintendents in these terms, of course, but I was undeterred, allowing my vision to emerge slowly and hoping there'd be an opportunity to make it real.

I was inspired by a handful of school district leaders like Marcus Foster, highly respected in Oakland, California, where he negotiated in a volatile environment with groups of various political orientations to raise the success of students in the minority-majority schools. Tragically, he was murdered before he could realize his vision. Another superintendent who inspired me was Forbes Bottomly, the Seattle School District Superintendent, a true visionary who served from 1965 to 1973, a time when the district was desegregating the schools, dealing with growing economic problems, and changing teaching philosophies and methods. He was a major focus of my dissertation.[10] In the archives of the Suzzallo Library at the University of Washington, I found a lengthy white paper with actual blueprints for radically different designs for schools intended for Seattle's Central District. The civil rights' wars of the era had prevented him from bringing his vision to fruition, but what I learned from his words and drawings was both inspiring and quite possible.

My interview with Dr. Bottomly felt authentic. A true gentleman, gifted in intellect and flush with courage and heart, he was candid about the challenges he had faced in the community, as he shared his insights into the machinations of district politics. From his obituary in the *Seattle Times*, I learned that he had built his own boat and made many long journeys far into the Pacific Ocean. His former colleagues wanted his epitaph to read, "He was a visionary leader whose efforts greatly improved the educational opportunities and experiences of thousands of children." But Bottomly chose these words instead: "He was a master boatwright."

I became a superintendent in an era when, at best, superintendents were implementers-in-chief—not visionary leaders like Drs. Foster and Bottomly. A true vision—best expressed as an image or a phrase—inspires others to try new approaches because they feel ownership. An authentic vision is a shared experience, crafted by many hands.

This all had to wait when I became Superintendent of Bainbridge Island School District in 1997. Bainbridge Island, Washington, was a charming and well-educated community across Puget Sound from Seattle—part rural, part small town, and part suburban ferry commuters. I felt lucky to be in district and community with such appeal to me. But once I began my job, I had little time to enjoy my new community. There were new management practices to be installed and new administrative personnel to hire. Many parents liked the schools as they were, and the kids already measured high in academic performance. As soon as I arrived, some school board members told me through off-handed comments how to run things as they sought fit. And they wanted me to know how much the community liked its schools as they were. I took the subtext to be: don't make waves. For most administrators, that would have been fine. Safe choices and conviviality could have been the keys to being there a long time, probably into retirement. But I had too much Mr. G, A.S. Neill, and Forbes Bottomly in my veins to remain placid when change was so sorely needed.

Before I was hired, the Bainbridge Island community had approved a bond to build a new school. They had acquired centrally located land adjacent to the middle school; and the grade level designation had not yet been made. Any choice—expanding the high school by a grade level or realigning neighborhood boundaries for all three elementaries—would have repercussions, and I understood that.

I assembled an advisory team to review each choice and its consequences. I entertained another option as well, to create a grades 5-6 intermediate school whose program would be geared to the special needs of ten-to-twelve-year-old children who were developmentally too old for elementary school yet too young for middle school, where we could have a one-teacher classroom in the first year and team teachers in their second year. I knew it would require a design process with a yet-unnamed planning principal, and we would need to find a progressive architect who would allow us to design the program before completing their drawings. Although I'm not an architect, I do know that form should follow function, and I knew this would be one of the keys to the school's success.

At the time, an intermediate grades school was a relatively new concept. I saw it as an innovative school in the midst of a small, traditional system. My challenges were hiring a crackerjack planning principal, identifying the right architect, and eventually hiring or transferring in teachers who were eager to try a new way of schooling. As is usually the case when a vision has firm roots, I just knew the pieces would fall into place. It was a dream that, for me, had already come true even before we broke ground for the new building.

I knew the school would need a symbolically powerful name that spoke to the Bainbridge Island community and its history. I had already established relationships with the Bainbridge Island Japanese American Community (BIJAC)—nearly all the parents, as children, had been sent to internment camps in Manzanar and Minidoka following President Roosevelt's Executive Order 9066. Americans of Japanese ancestry on Bainbridge Island and throughout the West Coast and Hawaii were displaced from their homes, land, and businesses, allowed to take only what they could carry. This racist atrocity was a wound that cut deeply through the Bainbridge Island community and its history.

In my quiet discussions with Don Nakata, the head of BIJAC and a widely respected community leader, we recognized an exciting opportunity to name the new school. I did not need to be sold on the importance of naming the school after a Japanese American family. But which one? The School Board was wise enough to assemble an advisory committee with at least one or two Japanese American parents and teachers to make a recommendation.

The School Board approved naming the school for Sonoji and Yoshiko Sakai. Sonoji was *issei*, a first-generation immigrant. In 1918 he purchased land and started a farm. Later, he sold part of his land to the school district, the very site where the new school would be built. His eldest daughter, Kay Sakai Nakao, became the family's emissary and historian for the school. Until her death at age 100, she was actively engaged with events and rituals that kept the Sakai name and traditions alive. It is to the credit of the school's first principal, Jo Vander Stoep, and her staff, that Sakai Intermediate embodied a student-centered culture that lives on today.

My role in helping create the vision of Sakai Intermediate School and handing it off to a dynamic principal and staff was the signal success of my career. Nothing in all my years of working with schools would ever mean this much to me. I knew that all the lessons I'd learned along the way had infused me with the spirit and leadership to pull it off.

At the twenty-year reunion of the school's founding, which corresponded with Kay's 100th birthday, I asked her eldest son if I could share a word with him after the ceremony and celebration were over:

> My dad was a young naval doctor stationed in the Pacific Theater. He arrived in Hiroshima not long after the atomic bomb had leveled the city. In our family living room back in the Midwest, sitting for years on a bookshelf, were two mementos he brought home. One was small porcelain doll and the other was what my mother referred to as a Japanese Bible. Even though my folks never discussed these items, I knew what they represented, as each looked like a toasted

marshmallow on one side, having been scorched by the atomic blast and the fire that followed. These images are burned into my mind, and they continue to remind me of the horror of war and man's inhumanity to his fellow man. So, when I think of Sakai Intermediate School and my role in its creation, I like to think I have offered a small token, in the spirit of redemption, for the destruction our country leveled on the land of your ancestors. I think I was led to Bainbridge Island twenty years ago for that purpose, and it has been the honor of my life to do so.

Fate had taken me on a long, twisted path of sorrows and successes, which ultimately led me to Bainbridge Island, Washington. I was grateful that I could again build something important with others from a vision of developing a new school model, but this time, on a bigger scale. But my success on Bainbridge Island left me totally unprepared for what was to happen next. Little did I anticipate my "political assassination" in my next school district, nor its fateful role in my life's journey. That experience would be the harbinger of the dark night of my soul. And from that dark night, I would emerge a changed person.

PART SEVEN

Everybody deserves what they get,
whether they deserve it or not.
~ Issan Dorsey, Roshi, Zen Buddhist teacher ~

28. A Bridge Too Far

I was flattered to be contacted by a partner of the pre-eminent recruitment firm for placing superintendents into major school districts. The Bainbridge School Board had decided not to renew my contract—citing financial deficits as the reason—and I was more than ready to move on.

I knew leaving would be difficult for Johanna and Eddie. They had adjusted well to Bainbridge Island and really had no reason to move. Johanna liked her job teaching gifted elementary students in a neighboring school district, and Eddie had good friends and was gaining notoriety for his many acting and singing performances at Bainbridge Performing Arts. We sensed then that he might have a future in theater. He was completing his first year of middle school and this was not the best time to uproot a teen. Of all people, I should have known better.

The firm promoted a job in Sunnyvale, California, which ironically was Johanna's hometown. Her parents still lived in the house she grew up in, and their health was declining. The Fremont Union High School District (FUHSD) was a prestigious school district, comprised of five high-performing high schools that sprawled across Cupertino, Sunnyvale, and parts of San Jose and Los Altos. It was a well-funded school district. Due to its high property tax base, it was, like its neighbor Palo Alto, one of a few California school districts that did not rely only on state funding. It was able to pocket the difference between state revenues and what it gained from property taxes. The teachers' union contract allowed a direct flow of these funds to compensation. I had never heard of a salary agreement that was so beneficial to teachers and other employees. I thought negotiating union contracts was one issue I could take off my plate. But that rosy prospect soon changed.

The district was a majority-minority school district in which racial minority groups comprise a majority of the district's population, which included people with family and cultural ties to China, Taiwan, Southeast Asia, India, Korea, Japan, Iran (Persia), Mexico, and Central America.

Central office administration was stable, well-compensated, and decidedly bureaucratic. Each central office administrator and principal ruled his or her department or school as a fiefdom. Despite its entrenched ways, the district seemed like a good opportunity and potential steppingstone to something bigger once Eddie graduated. Johanna would be closer to her parents, and I would be in the backyard of Stanford once again.

A voice in my head told me I had been a superintendent once and there was no point in doing it again. What I really wanted was a new creative challenge, *but I ignored that voice*. Johanna also warned me after the FUHSD School Board paid a visit to the Bainbridge School District and to our home: "You're going to have trouble with the tall Asian woman. She's suspicious of you. She doesn't like you, even though she doesn't know you. I can't tell what her issue is, but she's going to be difficult to deal with. How badly do you want this job?"

It was hubris on my part. I had routinely dealt with difficult people. I was comfortable in my skin as a white man working in a multicultural context. And the compensation package was more than double what it had been in Bainbridge, plus the FUHSD Board threw in a $500,000 loan toward buying a home. I accepted the job and flew to District headquarters to sign my contract and be interviewed by the *San Jose Mercury News*. The selection process, which had been designed by the same Chicago consulting firm, had been conducted behind closed doors to this point. No candidates were known to the public. There had been no opportunity for staff and community to have input into the process. I was the mystery man. This was the beginning of my bumpy initiation.

The current School Board President arranged for me to meet the soon-to-be retired Superintendent and his senior Cabinet members. I knew little of him and he knew nothing of me. His Executive Secretary ushered me into his office and indicated that he would join me shortly. I was astonished to find that three walls of his office were covered with mirrored glass tiles, from the ceiling to the floor. My brain quietly exploded with *WTF?!* Before I could fully take in this most peculiar office, the Superintendent entered in a brusque manner, hesitating only to touch my hand in a limp handshake. He didn't mince words and got right to it.

"No one knows who you are or how you got this job. The Cabinet is furious with the School Board and with you. Several of these people should have been my successor. The whole process stinks. Okay, now let's meet them." And with that, he opened a side door to his office and vanished. Like a line of ducklings, the Cabinet members filed in and remained standing. Holy shit! I hadn't felt this taken aback since Jean met me at the door with, "I didn't ask for you to come. What gives you the right?"

Noticing a small conference room next to his office, I asked if we might sit down so I could briefly introduce myself. I may have looked unperturbed, but my mind was whirling out of control. I needed to compose myself, but there was no time. My only recourse was to take on the issue directly. This was my first test—and my contract hadn't even begun.

"I understand that you all are pissed off with the Board, and probably with me too, for the way the search process was conducted. I had no say in any of it. I understand many of you are well-qualified for the job and it's understandable that you are upset for not having a chance to interview with the Board. I would feel the same way. I acknowledge and respect your loyalty to the District and to yourselves, and I hope, in time, you can work with me."

I could sense a subtle shift in the vibe, even though most of them remained expressionless. I then shared a little of my background in nearby Redwood City and Stanford, and I stated that my wife's parents lived only two miles away and that she was a graduate of the former Buchser High School in neighboring Santa Clara. I thought my local connections might give me credibility, and I concluded with a quick statement about my belief in vision and the importance of collaborative leadership. My time was up, and I still couldn't get read on them.

The Executive Secretary scooted them out and announced that a small lunch was being brought to me before my interview, after which I would sign my contract. On cue, the Cabinet members rose in unison, shook my hand one by one, and silently left the room. Once alone, I tried to collect my wits. I had pitted my dress shirt, and my hands were trembling after what felt like a matinée performance at Kabuki Theater. Soon after, there was quiet knock on the door. Two of the Cabinet members looked a little wrung-out and a bit sheepish. Then the woman I eventually would name as my Deputy Superintendent spoke up.

"We just wanted you to know that we like how you handled yourself and what you had to say. You are a very different person than the current Superintendent. We understand why the School Board doesn't want anyone from the Cabinet even to apply. It would just be more of the same. You are not more of the same. We just wanted to tell you that we don't know where you will lead us, but we are ready to follow."

I was heartened by their faith in me, but the others were entrenched bureaucrats—mostly male cronies in safe positions. I was an outsider and a threat to their grip on the status quo. That dynamic was not going away. But schools would open soon and there was work to be done. As the new school year began, the School Board had a new President: the woman Johanna had warned me about. My wife's intuition turned out to be prophetic.

As is common with most superintendents and their board presidents, we met twice monthly, prior to each School Board meeting, to review the upcoming agenda, which was my task to put together. She could barely follow the agenda or understand the difference between an action item and an issue for discussion, and her demeanor from our very first one-on-one meeting was suspicious, harboring vague accusations.

What should have taken an hour became three-hour harangues with unsubstantiated claims of hers about my hidden motives and secret deals. And things only got worse from there. After several meetings, she accused me of unspecified maleficence and skullduggery. She made claims that I was lying to the Board, without any evidence, but there was nothing that I could say to change her mind. She was putting me on notice who held the reins of power on the School Board and in the School District. Her stunt was as laughable as it was inappropriate. I saw it as another test and knew I needed to establish the authority of my position without throwing more gasoline on to the fire of her ranting. I had to draw a line if I were to preserve my integrity and get any school district business done. I had learned my lesson at the picket lines at the University of Wisconsin.

I told her she was free to disagree with me, but I refused to be treated in this matter. I told her to stop or I would ask her to leave my office. She didn't, so I showed her door and said I wanted to take this incident and her behavior directly to the Board in closed session. As you may surmise, people can get fired for what I did, whether justified or not. I knew full-well that her behavior and my unwillingness to capitulate would only deepen our mutual antagonism. I saw no end to the toxicity of my relationship with her. After she left, I made a call to my attorney, Greg McCoy, who one day would feel like my best and only friend. Together, we began to chronicle what became a long and deteriorating relationship with her and two other Board members who eventually conspired behind the scenes to take me out.

The catalyst for my ongoing difficulties began a month into my tenure with the Silicon Valley dot-com bubble crash of October 2002. The precipitous loss of property tax revenues hit us full square in January. Our projected revenue loss exceeded $10 million. We began by laying off classified employees. Due to the teacher union contract, we were also able to cut salaries to close our budget deficit. We eventually cut six percent of the salaries of all employees including my senior staff and me. This was not much of a way to start my first year in the job, but it had to be done.

I had heard rumors that a large number of students were attending our schools whose parents did not live within School District boundaries. If true, these students were freeloading off taxpaying families whose hefty property taxes were the source of District revenues. This meant that if those false-residency students were dropped from our roles, we could potentially save millions, maintain teacher positions, and keep class sizes in check. This could become our salvation. With much public debate and the reluctant approval of the School Board, we moved forward with a plan to disenroll all students for the coming year and require all families to provide proof of residency to enroll their children for the coming school year. This was the only way to weed out those with false residency credentials from actual residents inside school district boundaries.

As we were to learn, the bulk of nonresident students had been attending three of our schools with the highest test scores, the schools with the highest percentage of Asian students. In the coming months, we discovered neighbors selling the use of their mailboxes and home addresses in preferred school areas for $5,000 a year, in order to help parents falsely register their children. We found evidence of cramped apartments that housed several students living on their own, while their parents lived in Taiwan. There was growing evidence that we had large scale fraud in our midst. And it was painfully obvious that the frenzy to get into our highest performing schools was strictly based on reputation and high-test scores. As I got to know many students, it was shocking to hear of the pressure they were under, less from their teachers than their parents. In many Taiwanese and mainland Chinese families, nothing less than perfection was acceptable. That's not a negative stereotype. That's a fact.

All hell broke loose after we notified parents of the new residency requirements. Long lines of parents were seen at the School District Office, waiting to re-enroll their child, to protest, or to present further false identification. The outrage by some of the aggrieved parents spread into a protest movement aimed chiefly at me. Quietly, many in the community supported the rationale for our new policies, and teachers understood what was at stake for them. The racial tension running through this conflict was palpable. What was presented publicly by angry parents as moral outrage was a cover for sanctimony and privilege. Some parents and community members would do whatever it took to preserve their sense of superiority and entitlement that comes with that power.

The conflict over the new residency policy came to the attention first of the *Wall Street Journal*, who sent a reporter to interview others and me, investigating claims that it was a racist contrivance aimed at Asian kids. The *WSJ* also asked about the growing numbers of white families who were moving away from schools in Cupertino because of the growing Asian hegemony in the community—an allegation I profusely denied, even though I knew it was true. The ABC news magazine show *20/20* also came to film the long lines and interview me via satellite. I don't recall what I said, but I'm sure it was as bland as possible, as anything I might say would have drawn more attention. For several weeks, there was a persistent focus on what we were doing, with repeated stories on local TV news and in the *San Jose Mercury News*.

By the time school started, enrollment had dropped by seven hundred students in a district of roughly ten thousand. This was a victory and vindication for us, as we restored salary cuts that year and made salary increases in the following year. But despite the unprecedented measures we took to solve our financial crisis, I should have known my goose was cooked. I had enemies, including the three members of my Board who were plotting my overthrow. The way it ultimately happened, however, sprang from another issue related to the then School Board President.

At the school year's end in 2006, one of the principals in the school district reassigned a teacher at her school to a counseling position, not realizing that one of the other counselors carried a grudge against this teacher. The counselor with the grudge was wife of the current Board President, a Mr. Levinson. The newly assigned counselor had found the Levinsons' daughter guilty of cheating in his class a few years earlier. It had happened and was over, not that big a deal I thought, but it was surely not over for Board President Levinson.

A day after the transfer came to my attention, Mr. Levinson, an otherwise obsequious fellow, stormed into my office to demand that I rescind the transfer for reasons he would not reveal. I told him the principal was allowed to do this within the collective bargaining agreement and therefore neither he nor I could interfere. I would, I told him, get further legal guidance and bring it to the Board as a whole if need be. "I want this done," he snapped back at me within earshot of several others. "I want this transfer cancelled, and I have the authority to tell you to do it. If you don't, I have the votes to get you fired."

There it was, bold as the noonday sun. Saying he had the votes meant he had already been working behind the scenes, presumably with the two Board members who'd had it in for me, which was not only unnerving but patently illegal. According to California's sunshine law (the Brown Act), local government business must be conducted in open and public meetings except in certain limited circumstances.

Word spread in the community about how the Board President and his wife were blackballing a very popular teacher. This young teacher subsequently met with the Deputy Superintendent, who encouraged him to apologize to Mrs. Levinson to soften her lingering animosity. Instead, he resigned and moved out of state, further inflaming the school's parents and students. Now the Board President was the target for community animosity, not me.

In the midst of this fracas, I inadvertently made matters worse. Before the teacher's resignation, I sent an email to my Deputy to express my disgust with the Board President, as rumor after rumor spread about his intent to get me fired. I don't recall my words, but they, in effect, expressed my strong desire that the Board President resign. I then *inexplicably* cc'd the whole Board. Freudian or not, what a slip!

The School Board meeting following the teacher's resignation began in closed session without me, a sure sign something was up. Sitting nearby in the hallway, I could see large numbers of parents and students filing into the large Board Room to express their anger at Levinson. The scene was bizarre, like a bad dream.

As the School Board members filed out of closed session, I caught the eye of the two Board members who had steadfastly supported me. They looked shaken, if not shocked, by what had just happened. Before we could approach each other, Levinson grabbed my arm, like a bailiff escorting an unruly observer out of court. With a snarl of retaliation in voice, he told me, "The Board has taken a vote to fire you. We will vote again on that measure in public session. You have five minutes to get your things and clear your desk. Leave your phone and your computer. You are no longer allowed in the building."

And that was it. It happened so quickly I simply couldn't register it in my brain. I didn't feel anger. My senses shut down, and I was numb. Only later did I recognize that when I left the building, I would never see or hear from anyone in the School District again, save my Deputy and one of the principals who became a superintendent elsewhere in California. I had hired over forty administrators of my sixty-member administrative team. I felt a closeness and a loyalty to each of them. They apparently were told by the School Board's attorney not to contact me. Hence, there was no goodbye and no closure. I feel saddest (and rather resentful) about not being able to connect with my colleagues one last time. Being barred from closure was another layer of indecency to the whole ugly affair.

There was an exception to the no-contract rule imposed on me. A day later, while I was nursing a hangover from too many gins and tonics, my former Deputy, now Acting Superintendent, called me with the Director of Finance listening on the line.

"I'm afraid we have more bad news. The School Board has decided not to honor the severance stipulations in your contract, even though you have been released for No Cause. I am authorized to pay you for the six days you worked in August, plus your remaining vacation days. I know this sounds unfair, and I am sorry. I can't say or do any more than that." That was it—the loss of eighteen months of pay and the loss of retirement contributions, the financial cushion I should have enjoyed to buffer against the calamity that was at my doorstep. That was a lot of money and a big piece of my family's financial future, which were legally due to me.

This time I didn't feel numb; I felt enraged. I remember yelling at them on the phone about how ugly and unfair my termination was. I felt like I had been ambushed—assassinated. Moreover, I felt betrayed by my Deputy, whose loyalty and friendship I thought had meaning for both of us. After all, I helped break the glass ceiling for her in the all-boys world of the School District's culture. I have often wondered what I would have done if the tables had been turned? Would I have stood up to the School Board if they fired her as a similar clown-act of revenge? Would I have staked my career on the values I believed in? Or did she support the Board to assure her ascendance to the superintendency or perhaps do what she could to protect the School District from its own School Board? I'll never know. Regardless of her motives, I felt betrayed by her. *Et tu, Brute?* It was all too much to bear.

Beyond the personal betrayal, I felt searing public humiliation. Upon the advice of my attorney, I declined to publicly comment on the details of what had really happened between Levinson and me. I was unable to defend myself in the ongoing reportage by the *Mercury News*. The School Board eventually sponsored an independent investigation, but this came to naught, as the very same three Board members who voted to fire me redacted all the evidence from the investigation report that pointed to their plot and illegal activities.

The hard truth was that no one, aside from my attorney and my immediate family, knew or cared about any of it. I was there one minute and gone the next. It felt like Orwell's *1984*: "History has stopped. Nothing exists except an endless present in which the Party is always right.

Latent feelings of rejection and abandonment triggered rage, humiliation, and grief. My spirit was broken, and other than my wife, I had no one to turn to. I should have seen a therapist for help, but my shame was so great I just wanted to hide from the world. I chastised myself by thinking my depression and feelings of helplessness were character flaws. I beat myself up for being so stupid. I should have listened to my wife and my inner voice before I took the job. I should have seen all this coming. I should have applied for another job when I still had the opportunity. Was my ego so invested in prevailing over the School Board that I put my family's security at risk? These voices kept me awake for years to come.

While writing this memoir, I came across this quote from poet David Whyte:

> To run from vulnerability is to run from the essence of our nature; the attempt to become something we are not and, most especially, to close off our understanding to the grief of others. More seriously, in refusing our vulnerability we refuse the help needed at every turn of our existence and immobilise the essential, tidal, and conversational foundation of our identity.[11]

After being fired, I did run from my very nature. I locked myself in my own prison cell to avoid further public humiliation. Rather than seek help, I chose to stay hidden until fate revealed another pathway. I eventually sued the Fremont Union High School District for wrongful termination and damages. Although I prevailed in mediation seven months later. I settled for much less than my attorney and I expected. Unfortunately, I soon discovered I was unemployable. I applied for over a hundred positions throughout California but interviewed for only a few. I had sued a school board. That I was vindicated was irrelevant. I was radioactive and my career as I knew it was over.

It took two years before I finally got a job back in Washington State. I moved there and lived alone in Seattle for two more years, while Johanna and Eddie stayed in the Bay Area. Eddie was accepted to California School of the Arts (CalArts) in Valencia, where he majored in Theater. After he graduated, he moved to North Hollywood and eventually began his career in sketch comedy, music video production, and animatics video editing. Johanna took a great job with the New Teacher Center in Santa Cruz. Despite my own glum circumstances, nothing could have made me happier than to see them do what they did best and with such joy.

29. The Dalai Lama, Sharon Stone, and Me

Whatever professional ambitions I had held for myself were dead, as was my confidence. The pain of the primal wound that develops when a mother and child are separated by adoption shortly after childbirth came back at me with a vengeance. Even though I enjoyed the love and loyalty of my wife and son, I felt cut off from the world. The shattering of my dream at age fifty-seven was not much different from losing my knee when I was sixteen. I was past wondering about my identity: *Who am I?* Now I wanted to know: *Why me?*

In the two years before moving back to Seattle, with no answers and no prospects for work, I slipped into a mundane daily routine, sulking all the while. While Johanna readied herself for work each morning, I would drink coffee, scan the *Mercury News*, peruse the professional want ads, prepare a shopping list for dinner, and take a long bike ride or go for a swim. Later, I'd go to a local coffee shop, usually with a book and writing journal in hand, stare out the window, and compose a poem or two. Mostly, I would simply watch people go about their business, seemingly without a care in the world. In the evenings, I would drink jug chardonnay and immerse myself in reruns of *Gunsmoke* and *Monty Python's Flying Circus*. I also was transfixed by *The Power of Myth* with Joseph Campbell and Bill Moyers from my DVD collection. Something about this program mesmerized me. Myths and the many images used to express them felt restorative, as if I were able to fuse my imagination with these cultures and tales, which happily were distant in time and space. Admittedly, the chardonnay helped.

One day my routine was interrupted by a call from Tom Thorning, inviting me to play golf with him at a fundraiser for the Dalai Lama Foundation, which he had helped found. I was one of the honored guests at the evening banquet that followed, which was a welcome respite from my problems with the school board

Apparently, the Chancellor of the local community college thought I was doing something right as many of my school district's high performing students funneled to her college At a silent auction before dinner, I found a table with a *Golf Digest* photo of Lama Kunga Rinpoche, one of the first lamas the Dalai Lama sent to the US, in a sand trap holding a wedge, with the heading "Good Karma, Bad Golf." *Who wouldn't spend $500 to play eighteen holes with a Tibetan Lama,* I thought? It was a no-brainer. I bid on and won a round of golf with Lama Kunga. I left that banquet walking on air!

Several weeks later, my round of golf with the Lama Kunga, Tom, and another friend was a sheer delight. Tom and I chuckled that no one cursed that day, which is rather exceptional for a golf outing. Lama Kunga played well for a man in his mid-seventies. He was generous and inviting, and he had a sparkly sense of humor. His putting was a little off that day; and I admit I was somewhat surprised that he took several three-foot gimmes. But I certainly was not going to question him for taking whatever gimmie he wanted. After all, he was a highly venerated spiritual being. And I was an average duffer who celebrated breaking a hundred.

As I was to learn, Tibetan Buddhists are pragmatic and disciplined, but they also emanate a subtle, divine spirit. I learned that if you hang with them for a while, their humor and spiritual insight will inevitably bubble up. I experienced this with Lama Kunga at the end of our round of golf at the 19th Hole over chilled cans of Diet Pepsi. He invited me to ask him a question, and I mumbled something about "beginner's mind," hoping I didn't appear to be a bigger dope than I already thought I was in his presence.

I forget how he answered my question about the fundamental Zen Buddhist precept of beginner's mind, but with a twinkle in his eye, he gently patted the back of my still-sweaty hand with both his palms. I could feel a palpable shift—an opening—in the space that was ours alone in that moment. I felt at ease with him and myself. Somehow, I understood that words were not necessary, yet he spoke briefly about being patient with myself. There was no doubt that he opened me with his warm heart, just so I could see the world and myself with forgiveness. In that moment, I could feel the walls of my isolation begin to dissolve. I could see that it was me—not the School Board or my former deputy—who was responsible for my bitterness and my sense of futility about life itself.

We sat together in silence a while longer in the shade of a large California live oak tree as the sun began to set over the cliffs to the west. There was nothing to do but inhale the fine fragrance of eucalyptus and watch the thin clouds pass above our heads like nameless thoughts traversing an imagined mind. It would take time for me to realize that Lama Kunga was transmitting his dharma to me, and at of all places, an upscale country club in Carmel Valley. It happened with such effortless grace that I barely felt a thing.

A few months later, Tom invited me see the Dalai Lama himself at the historic Pasadena Playhouse for a three-day lecture and commentary on the texts of Nāgārjuna, the second great Buddha. Nāgārjuna put forth the critical teachings of the *dependent origination*, which, from a lay perspective, means that there is no separate anything. There is no independent origination of anything. Everything is dependent on everything else. This state of perpetual dependence is total existence, a closed system so to speak. There is no separateness of one thing, or even one idea, from another. Time and space are indistinguishable.

On day two, I was invited to a private reception for the Dalai Lama in a meeting room in a large Pasadena hotel. It was a small group, but it also was a big celebrity affair. I thought I saw Monty Python's John Cleese wandering in the outer corridor, while singer k.d. lang hung back in a corner trying desperately not to be noticed. Hollywood actress Sharon Stone sat next to Tom on the dais while the Dalai Lama warmly greeted old and new friends. He regaled the audience with stories about how much better he felt since his bowels had started to function again, after getting very sick in India. I guess this proved that anyone, even an enlightened being, can have intestinal troubles in India. He was delightfully graphic about his primary orifices and how they work in harmony when one is well. He was hilarious and had the gathered dignitaries in stitches. I found him to be very direct in a nonchalant manner—completely endearing, as anyone who has ever seen him would say.

Then he launched into a soliloquy about whether he would name his successor before his death or just end the lineage, making the fourteenth Dalai Lama the last one. Even though it seemed he was worried about what the Chinese would do after his death, he refrained from any negativity about the Chinese military that had overrun Tibet when he was a young man and, in many ways, continue to do so. In 1959, the Chinese Communists destroyed thousands of Buddhist monasteries and killed or imprisoned over a million of his countrymen. Like so many Buddhists of his generation, he uttered not a harsh word nor a hint of recrimination. What an example for the world to learn from.

While he was talking, Sharon Stone sat erect with her hands folded in a mudra. Her face contorted, as her eyes rolled back in her head. It was hard for me not to laugh out loud. Her demeanor was a complete dichotomy compared with the charming Tibetan guy in robes sitting next to her, who was just being himself. The moment was unforgettable.

When gorgeous blond Sharon Stone, dressed in a short skirt, is seated just ten feet away and two feet above you on a stage, her bare legs parallel to your line of sight, it's hard not to think of her in *Basic Instinct*. I was in a state of jaw-dropping wonder. For just a moment, in my private universe, it was just the Dalai Lama, Sharon Stone, and me.

I got to know Sharon a little better at events in Los Angeles, Irvine, and San Francisco. I came to like her when she wasn't too busy being famous—when she seemed to be just herself. She was a good ambassador for Buddhism, despite the fact that she didn't come across as someone trying to shed her ego. If she had, her movie stardom surely would have evaporated. That would have been a loss. Her situation was similar to a story Tom told me about Richard Gere, who reportedly told the Dalai Lama he wanted to quit acting and devote himself completely to Buddhism. The Dalai Lama replied, "You can't stop being an actor! You're Richard Gere. That is who you are. I'm the Dalai Lama. I can't quit being the Dalai Lama, it's who I am. Stick to who you are."

I still feel a bit sad for movie stars like Sharon Stone and Richard Gere. I wonder if the gift of their celebrity is its own curse—being walled off behind an invisible shield that separates them from others, and perhaps from themselves. On the other hand, maybe this is true of many of us, minus the stardom.

Sharon was the emcee at the Inaugural Gala for the Missing Peace Project at UCLA's Fowler Cultural History Museum in late 2006. Again, the high-profile affair was a mix of Hollywood celebrities, world-famous artists, and Tibetan Buddhist luminaries. The art show was a collection of art pieces in various media, celebrating the Dalai Lama. Geshe Tsultim Gyeltsen was the honored guest. He made a short speech with the help of a translator before the guests were welcomed to view the spacious gallery. Sharon stood beside him as he bestowed a prayer shawl to each of us before entering. As in the case of Lama Kunga, he took my hand and held it for some time before placing a prayer shawl across my shoulders. I was so happy that Johanna and Eddie were with me that evening. I still have that shawl and I still remember the softness of his hands on mine. I felt this was another invitation to open my heart—an encouragement to bow with gratitude to the divine spirit that surrounds us. Nothing needed to be said. I understand that now.

The biggest surprise of those three days with the Dalai Lama in Pasadena was the dream I had the night after his private reception. I dreamed of him dressed in traditional maroon and gold, but instead of a robe, he wore the uniform of an emergency medical technician (EMT). He held a small human form wrapped in his uniform, like a parent holding a baby in a blanket. He lifted this childlike form, all swaddled up, and put it in my arms. He then placed his hands on my temples—like *Star Trek's* Dr. Spock's Vulcan mind-meld. Suddenly, from his body, arms, and hands, a radiant light enveloped me. After that, I woke up—breathless, with my eyes ablaze. *What just happened?* I was on fire with golden light.

In the morning, I raced to find Tom and some of his foundation buddies near the door of the Playhouse's Green Room. I was hyperventilating as I hurriedly described my miraculous dream. One of the co-founders of the foundation looked at me with a sly grin, chuckled, and seemed on the edge of pitying me. "Hey, don't you get it? That's the way he works, stupid. He's fond of using dreams that way. It's his way of waking you up."

I didn't know how to react. I sensed a little condescension, but what did I know? I thought better of it for a second, as I considered that I might have been initiated to something far bigger than I could imagine. But to what?

30. Out of the Labyrinth

The benefit of wallowing in two depressing years of unemployment was that I had the time to find myself, outside the labyrinth in which I'd been lost. Even though I often sat in my office hoping for solace to come my way in the form of a job offer, a subtle sense of ease began to trickle up in my soul. Not every day was drudgery and sameness. Eventually, I returned to interests that stretched back to my teens, such as reading pioneering psychologists and theologians. I also began studying the works of Pema Chödön, Jack Kornfield, Adyashanti, and other contemporary spiritual leaders. I not only regained my appreciation for poetry, I began to write again.

I attended a book reading by poet Jane Hirshfield in San Jose, just as her book *Come, Thief* was released. After her reading, I dashed to the head of the book-signing line and had a brief and inspired chat with her. A Buddhist herself, she got a kick out of hearing about the Dalai Lama, Sharon Stone, and the conundrum of reincarnation that I experienced in Pasadena. I also told her I was renewing myself as a poet. Without hesitation, she took her new book from my hand and inscribed these words:

> *To Steve—*
> *Open the window six inches more than is comfortable.*
> *The gate to poetry.*
> *Jane Hirshfield*

I was so touched by her thoughtfulness and her words. Through her beautifully crafted style, she transmitted some intangible connection to a poetic way of knowing the world and expressing how it makes us aware of its presence. When I got home later that evening, I found the words in "Fifteen Pebbles" that she had read aloud earlier:

> On the dark road, only the weight of the rope.
> Yet the horse is there.

Like her inscription to me, her sparse choice of words communicated a way of that knowing—a simple way of being still—the very essence of Zen, utterly grounded.

My dual interests in Zen and writing were fused in several weeklong writing retreats I attended with Natalie Goldberg in fascinating places like Sedona, Taos, and Ferme de Villefavard in the Limousin region near Limoges, France. She held these writing retreats like formal Zen retreats—no talking among fellow attendees except during class time when we could share samples of our work and ask her questions. The focus of her approach is on the practice of writing, not learning how to write better. Our many meditations sessions through the day helped calm our minds— settle our monkey-minds, as she would say—to reduce the noise in our heads so the beauty of what we were writing could flow through us.

I attended these retreats over several years, beginning just before the mediation of my lawsuit was settled. During this same time, I attended sessions and retreats with Adyashanti in Santa Cruz, Palo Alto, and Pacific Grove. These silent retreats with Natalie and Adyashanti could not have come at a better time. Through my experiences with them, I could at last feel an inner peace that had been elusive to me. My work with Natalie reinvigorated my love of writing and to listening to the words of others.

Perhaps my biggest breakthrough came with Adyashanti. One of his core tenets is the paradox of spiritual search. The more we pursue God or the next spiritual high, the more we take our attention away from the here and now. To be fully present, perhaps to experience a deeper form of awakening, we must give up searching to find what it is we think we are searching for. This paradox is much like a Zen kōan. It's not a puzzle to be solved but a vehicle that can only be understood outside the realm of rational thought. Like a moment of synchronicity that must come to us for understanding, this paradox of search is its own teacher and its own answer.

In the midst of all the turmoil and heartbreak that followed my firing, I felt like I was on a fast-track of deeper spiritual experience. Johanna and I saw Leonard Cohen at the Orpheum Theatre in Oakland. Sitting high in the balcony, I listened closely as Cohen briefly recounted his personal and professional reification, after spending five years in retreat at the Mount Baldy Zen Center near Los Angeles. It seemed clear that Cohen had come to the end of his personal rope before he took a time-out for those five years of Buddhist practice. Regarding his highly acclaimed tour, he quipped, "We began this tour three years ago. I was sixty years old—just a kid with a crazy dream."

As the crowd roared its approval, I shivered with the thought that my own reinvention might be possible. He then launched into his famed song "Anthem," singing these words with his deep, sonorous voice:

> Ring the bells that still can ring
> Forget your perfect offering
> There is crack in everything
> That's how the light gets in.

His words struck my heart. My tears flowed and my shoulders heaved, with little concern for whoever might see me in my dual state of grief and joy. As if hypnotized, I felt my soul take flight. All the negativity and hopelessness of my life were lifted. I could see a small figure in a prim dark suit and a neat fedora sing and dance across the stage far below. The rhythm and sway of "Anthem" played on. But for that moment, which seemed to have no end, I felt cradled in light. Like the title of one of Adyashanti's books, I felt I had *fallen into grace*.[12]

In the midst of this rich but restive period of my life, I began to question my fate from a new perspective. Had I, unknowingly, designed my own tumultuous fall? Had I unconsciously staged my firing—resulting in a humiliation so profound I could never recover from it? Maybe I *needed* this to happen. Maybe I needed to take a fall so big that I would be forced to radically divert from the life script I was blindly following. For that matter, had I somehow played an unconscious role in my athletic career-ending injury, allowing me to follow my interests in psychology and poetry instead of football? And if that were possibly the case, was the fate of my adoption something I had rendered before my birth? Were there some underlying truths that were still mine to be discovered?

I had been reading a lot of archetypal psychologist James Hillman's work. Even though his book *Re-visioning Psychology* was more than thirty years old at the time, it was fresh and relevant to me. But it was another of his books, *The Soul's Code,* that arrived at *just the right moment.* Hillman described the ancient idea that we choose the parents and the circumstances of our lives, after which we forget. The origin of this belief dates back to the Myth of Er retold in Plato's *Republic*. These are regarded as the soul's choices.

Hillman suggests that this myth "has a redemptive psychological function, and a psychology derived from it can inspire a life founded on it....[It] implies, we must attend very carefully to childhood to catch early glimpses of the daimon [fate or guardian angel] in action, to grasp its intentions and not block its way."[13] The myth of the daimon and the path of one's fate represent a *calling*. According to Hillman, "A calling may be postponed, avoided, intermittently missed. It may also possess you completely. Whatever; eventually it will out. It will make its claim."[14]

At that point in the train wreck of my life, something sure-as-hell had been making its claim on me. And I understood that accepting one's fate at face value would be a mistake. If getting into a horrible mess was part of my destiny, then getting out of it surely could be as well. I was utterly done with my insufferable suffering and the incessant whimpering whispers in my mind. My life depended on getting unstuck. But how?

It came to me in a dream. I had just read W. B. Yeats' poem "Among School Children." My dream seemed embedded in the poem.

I am a sixty-year-old smiling public man. I am in a schoolhouse deep in a dark forest, walking among school children who have been turned to porcelain, frozen in a hypnotic trance by a witch. I walk through another room and into a dense labyrinth, replete with dead-end pathways. In the far distance, beyond the labyrinth, I can see a tall spire atop a building that looks like a church. At the very peak of the spire is a flat metal sculpture shaped in a symbol of some kind. I don't know what it is, but in the dream, I realize this is my direction to head. This is my way out. Then I wake up.

The next day I called my good friend Dennis Flaherty, a highly respected Vedic astrologer in Seattle, to help me identify the symbol on the spire. He told me it was the astrological symbol for Mercury, or Hermes, the messenger of the gods and the guide of souls transiting between the Upper and Lower worlds. According to Joseph Campbell: "Hermes is the lord of the road to rebirth. He is the one who meets the soul at death and guides the path to eternal life of one kind or another. In that way, he is the lord also of roads, the protector of travelers."[15]

I knew my dream was prescient. I was being released from the grip of Hades and the Underworld to go into the light. A weight had been lifted.

In less than a week, I was called to interview at a school district near Seattle for the position of executive director of schools. I needed a job badly at this point, as our savings were exhausted. But in taking the job, our worlds turned upside down again. This transition was more abrupt than sad. Johanna quickly found a bungalow in Saratoga, California, only two blocks from where we were married. And I packed what I could cram into my SUV and headed to Seattle. We became a commuter couple for two years, which though not ideal, was perhaps good for us to take a break from the depressing grind of it all. Truth be told, she probably needed a break, and living apart was way better than living in the Underworld with me. I now was out of the labyrinth, beckoned by a mysterious symbol hanging above the horizon.

Unfortunately, escaping the labyrinth didn't pan out as I had hoped. It was more like a promotion from Hell to Purgatory. I was happy to have an income again, and enjoy good insurance benefits that allowed me to get my worn-out knee replaced. But I was a middle manager in a large school district, several levels below the superintendent, and it was hard to watch him do his job knowing I was equally capable of doing what he was doing. He and the men and women who formed his inner circle seemed singularly unexcited about new visions for schools. They lacked curiosity about innovative school models that were rapidly spreading in the charter school movement outside of Washington State. This was something I knew and cared a lot about, but my knowledge was of no use in that role. My district's agenda was all about improving student performance (i.e., test scores) in math and reading. I felt sad, as so much was at stake. The young people in our schools, who spoke over eighty languages at home, deserved better. They were due more respect than being treated as empty vessels into which knowledge could be poured like soft concrete oozing into foundation forms. Much of this knowledge was purchased as various instructional programs from expensive educational textbook companies, whose unspoken goals were to make curricula teacher-proof and their bottom lines stockholder-friendly.

As an unrepentant progressive educator, I was still in league with John Dewey, who said, "I believe finally, that education must be conceived as a continuing reconstruction of experience; that the process and goals of education are one and the same thing." While in this large school district, I was required to sniff the Kool-Aid of the standards-based movement. I'm just glad I never drank it.

After two years in that position, I left with great relief. I'd had more than enough. I returned to live with Johanna with hopes I might find a position in the Bay Area but no luck. Despite wanting to stay in California to be near Eddie, who was in Los Angeles, we could not afford to purchase a home in the Bay Area. Ultimately, we chose to move back to Bainbridge Island, where the cost of housing was comparatively low. We found a beautiful home at a time when the housing market was in the pits, and we moved in a matter of weeks. The Bay Area chapter of our lives and careers was over.

PART EIGHT

Life is not a problem to be solved,
but a mystery to be lived.
~ Joseph Campbell, Mythologist ~

31. Up in Flames

I was happy to be back on Bainbridge Island after a twenty-year hiatus. I was relieved to feel almost anonymous, although it was flattering to be recognized by the few who remembered me. I could blend in without being noticed at the Town and Country Market and the Blackbird Bakery. The culture of the Island suited me, as did the local attire of Gore-Tex jackets, low-cut Merrell walking boots, and faded jeans. No one cared what you drove, as every household had at least one beater—commonly referred to as their Island Car. Bainbridge Island, both a town and an island, was somewhere I could feel at ease with myself and others. I liked that Seattle was on the other side of Puget Sound. At home, our biggest problem was a small pack of coyotes who loved to howl at 3 a.m. on a regular basis. Even that was a treat, realizing that the many animals in our close-knit neighborhood seemed content to let us live in their forest.

It didn't take long before I got antsy though, as I didn't know what to do with my semi-retired life. Making a few extra dollars would be helpful, too, at least until Social Security payments began to flow, which would be a few years away. I needed to find a job and my best chance was on the Seattle side of Puget Sound. I knew that becoming a ferry commuter would add three hours of travel time, including driving and parking, but there are worse things in life—the views of Mount Rainier and Puget Sound from the large ferries were as calming as they were magnificent.

Sometimes you get what you ask for and I did. I landed two temporary jobs, one after the other, and both were miserable—or rather, I was miserable in them. I was chosen to be an Interim Chief Academic Officer in the most dysfunctional school district in the state. I thought I was familiar with it, but I didn't really check it out as I should have. I had to live the experience, it seems, to realize how bad it could be.

First, the district's one high school had gone through seven principals in six years. Second, the acting superintendent, who had no experience in the position, walked out the door without giving notice to the School Board two months before the end of her contract. I was asked by the School Board to assist with the search process for the next fool who thought they could tame the beast, which was the closest I've ever come to being a used-car salesman.

The following year I was drawn to a part-time position with an online university, where I supervised superintendent interns. This sounded appealing, as I would travel to the school district sites where the intern, often a central office administrator or principal, followed a menu of requirements to complete state certification. But it turned out that I could offer little leadership coaching, because their only requirement was to complete a checklist of administrative duties they were assigned by the state. I also monitored their progress in the required online courses. The more I observed, the more it seemed like a Ponzi scheme. Online universities such as this one reaped substantial income from high cost student tuition while maintaining a low overhead and paying low salaries for "professors" like me who simply monitored online course-taking and testing.

Midway through my second year, I was appointed to full professor for no apparent reason. My promotion came out-of-the-blue. I never went through a tenure process, nor did I receive a bump in salary or guaranteed employment. I was befuddled by the whole non-process-process, which no one, including the dean, could explain to me. Clearly, *the universe* was trying to send me a message: Get out or go insane!

The people I worked with were quite nice, even the ones I regarded as befuddled university administrators and instructors. So, I trudged through the job for two years, even after it was obvious that it was a mismatch for me. I was eventually "let go" due to enrollment decline, which I knew meant that the program was losing its appeal to aspiring administrators. I doubt that anyone missed me once I was out the door. In truth, I'm sure a few were glad to see me go. I'd had many run-ins with my superiors over what I perceived to be the idiotic machinations and threadbare curriculum of the school's online learning system.

I finally had my belly full of working for outfits like these. As Yogi Berra famously said, "It was déjà vu all over again."

Was I really such a misfit and crank? Even if I were, at this point I really didn't care. These experiences did little more than feed my cynicism and stoke the fire of my rebellion. I don't know why it took me so long to reach the end of my rope, but I was done trying to be seen and I was finished with trying to hold the reins of leadership. William James must have been undergoing his own moment like this when he wrote:

> I am done with great things and big plans, great institutions and big successes. I am for those tiny, invisible human forces that work from individual to individual, creeping through the crannies of the world like so many rootlets or like the capillary oozing of water, yet which, if given time, will rend the hardest monuments of human pride.[16]

159

I also was fed up with perseverating about the past, but I couldn't seem to shake the last drops of bitterness over being terminated in Silicon Valley. Johanna bore the brunt of my emotional quagmire. I pushed her patience too many times while I bounced from one frustrating job to another. My curmudgeonly moods were like black holes, capable of pulling anyone or anything in. I needed to do something to snap out of it, something major.

I hatched a scheme. On Christmas Eve 2013, our family huddled under the covered picnic shelter at Fay Bainbridge Park on the shores of Puget Sound. I had built a bonfire in the large stone fireplace. By the light of the fire, each of us read a poem about the Winter Solstice that I'd chosen. Unbeknown to them, I brought my last remaining file box of legal documents from my lawsuit against the Fremont Union High School District School Board. At my invitation, we took turns throwing reams of briefs and other documents into the fire, their sparks spiraling through the chimney into the sky. We also wrote wishes for each other for the future and threw those into the fire too. As a last touch, I pulled out a special bottle of Paso Robles Syrah from my pack and poured glasses for each of us to toast our family and welcome the New Year.

As the fire slowly turned to embers, we huddled together and reminisced about our many journeys since we left Bainbridge Island for California sixteen years earlier. When our energy began to wane, we silently watched the fire die down. It was well after dark, and no one was in the park but us. Puget Sound's dark waters barely rippled as there was no wind that evening. All we could see was the silhouette of the Seattle skyline in the distance. We stood in silence, taking it all in. The quiet reminded me of sitting with Lama Kunga under the oak tree in Carmel Valley.

The ritual I'd choreographed was based on initiation rites I had taken from Joseph Campbell. It was a simple ceremony of death and rebirth. I wanted to put my past to rest and welcome whatever might come next—hopefully something authentic and fulfilling. I had a ways to go, but burning my last legal files and letting go of resentments about that time made me think I'd made some progress after all.

Something special was set in motion that night, as though I had reached back in time to reclaim what had been lost or set aside in me. I recognized it as a vision I had of myself as a teen that, at long last, I was ready to bring it to life. I would become a psychotherapist, a dream I'd deferred for nearly half a century. Maybe the ceremony actually worked. It happened that quickly.

Over many years, my reading of psychology, mythology, and spirituality had kept the embers alive. During my two-year executive directorship near Seattle, I had seen a Jungian analyst who had trained in Zürich with luminaries like James Hollis and Murray Stein. On Bainbridge Island, I was seeing a local psychotherapist, Elizabeth Turner, who integrated Buddhism into her approach. Her guidance was instrumental in leading me to the Pacifica Graduate Institute near Santa Barbara, the only program in depth psychology with ties to Hillman, Campbell, and Jung.

The idea of going back to school was enticing, but the reality was another matter. I would be sixty-five when I enrolled; and when I graduated, sixty-eight. On top of that, I'd have to fly to Santa Barbara three weekends per quarter for ten quarters. The time and cost of travel alone seemed exorbitant.

Over lunch with an old friend. I yabbered at length about how much I would love to go back to school. This, I told her, was my dream from early teens. "Geez, Harriet. I'm too old for this, but I still I want to do it. The whole thing is calling me, but I just can't seem to jump off the diving board."

I heard myself say the words *just jump in*, and I flashed to Sanislo Elementary and Phil's simple advice for my first step in becoming a teacher. Just jump in. Before I could retrieve more of my memory of Sanislo, she responded: "Well, Steve. What's keeping you from doing it? What are you waiting for? This is who you were meant to be."

By the time I got back in my car, I knew there was no reason not to go to Pacifica. I had to jump in. What was I going to do with the rest of my life? I was hungry for a new kind of knowledge and new experiences that would hold my interest and perhaps help heal my battered soul. This was the way out of despair and possibly, the road to personal expression I'd been waiting for.

Going to Pacifica and getting licensed as a psychotherapist was about more than swapping one professional identity for another. I was seeking something bigger, a new way of being in the world. I was ready to explore new territories of the mind and the soul—to venture into the mysteries of life with *beginner's mind*. As Shunryu Suzuki, the founder of San Francisco Zen Center, once said, "In the beginner's mind there are many possibilities, but in the expert's there are few."[17]

I was done with experts and working for institutions. And I was definitely done with feeling like an orphan, unable to find a home. I was ready to become a beginner once again. This time, the goal was to become who I always was meant to be.

32. Records Unsealed

I made a quick trip to Iowa to visit my mother and Mr. G before starting my Master's program at Pacifica. On the day of my visit to see him at his country home, I detoured through Ottumwa to see if the American Home Finding Association was still there. Although I hadn't visited it before, I had corresponded with two successive directors for years, and it felt like an important stop on my journey.

I had rarely heard from my half-sisters Patty and Charlotte after Jean passed away, but I was still trying to find some unknown pieces of the puzzle of my life. Sure enough, the AHFA house was there, on a shaded residential street lined with large and well-mannered brick homes. A small sign marked the entrance. As I made my way unannounced through the front door, I found no main desk and no indication that anyone was around. Yet I felt welcome to walk into a large carpeted receiving room lined with couches and chairs, a large stone fireplace at the far end. A framed photograph of President Harry Truman caught my eye. The President appeared to be standing on the outdoor deck of a train depot. He had on his trademark Stetson hat and wore a wide grin on his face. He was shaking the hand of a young girl, perhaps four years old. It must have been winter, as both Truman and the girl wore heavy coats. The small plaque attached to the frame stated only: President Harry Truman, 1948.

A woman in her late fifties eventually entered the room and introduced herself as an assistant to the director. I explained who I was, and that I just wanted to get a look at the place from where I'd been adopted. She looked a little embarrassed, as she told me that the site of the original building was a few blocks away, where the student parking lot of Ottumwa High School now stood. This building was once the manse for the Episcopal Church across the street.

I asked if the director, Tom Lazio, had retired. "Oh my, no! He's still kicking. And might I say, I don't think he is a lot older than you! He's around here, but he's got a committee meeting of the City Council to get to. I doubt he has time to say more than hello. I'll get him."

I could hear heavy footsteps coming up from the basement, and then he appeared. I told him my name and reminded him of our correspondence over the years. "Good golly, of course I remember you, Steve. You wrote a letter for me to the Iowa Senate. I wish I could say things had improved, but not much has in that department."

I told him I knew he had to go soon, and that I had stopped by to ask if I could see my sealed records. I then told him a brief version of my tale of tracking down Gloria Jean Johnson.

163

"I've got a minute. Come into the mess I call my office."

He ushered me into a beautiful but cluttered room, which at one time must have been the Episcopal priest's private study. Stacks of books, papers, and files were scattered everywhere. I could barely see his desk. But then he got right to the point.

"We both know you are asking a lot. You can guess there still are restrictions on opening sealed files, which legally I cannot tamper with." But then he paused and rubbed his chin just before a sly grin lit up across his face. "You know, I've always said my job was putting families together, not taking them apart. I think your situation is unusual, as your birth mother is dead and no one has a clue about your birth father. He's probably dead too. Tell you what …" And with that he disappeared, and I could hear him descend into the basement. *What was he doing?*

After several minutes, he reentered his office carrying a bundle of musty manilla envelopes bound with an elastic cord.

I blurted out, "Is this it? Is this my sealed adoption record?"

It felt as if I had fallen into dream, as I watched him untie the bundle and peek into each envelope. He then pulled out a decorative card from one and held it up for me to see. It was an ink impression of my two little feet taken on the day I was born.

He then handed me the entire bundle and said, "I really do have to go in five minutes. Look at what you can now, and then I must have them back. Give them to Audrey. But I promise you, I will copy every single document and send those to you. Look for them in about a week. For now, it was my real pleasure to see you after all these years."

In turn, I took his hand and said, nearly blubbering, "Tom this is such a sweet gesture on your part. And the secret stays with me. I will never be able to thank you enough for today, let alone what you sent me twenty years ago. There never would have been a search without you."

With that, he was gone. And true to his request, I perused the files and handed them to his assistant. I thanked her as well. Before I left, I pointed to the picture on the wall of President Truman and the little girl.

"What's the story with that picture?"

"To my knowledge the President was on whistle-stop tour for the fall election. That's the old Ottumwa train depot and the girl was one of ours. I don't know why she was chosen. Given her age and the date of the picture, she may have been with us about the time you showed up. I don't know more than that. But it's telling, don't you think, that it's at the train depot? They were both going someplace, but in different directions. He was going back to the White House, and she, I don't know, I guess she was going where she was meant to be. That's fate for you."

The following week I received my records in the mail. I was more excited than a kid opening Santa's presents at Christmas. Much of what I found was familiar, but several documents changed the narrative of my adoption. My parents had applied for adoption eligibility nearly six months before they adopted me. And I wasn't legally adopted in June 1949, as I had thought, but in August 1950. I was on a year's trial run to see if I was a good match for them or if I had an undetected deficiency that would kill the deal. If that were the case, would they have returned me while still "under warranty"? Fortunately, my mother had sent effusive letters to the adoption agency assuring them that Bob and Ruth Rowley, and little Stevie, were getting on well.

Then came a bigger surprise. The documents showed that Jean had not entirely signed off on me ten days after my birth, as I thought. At the request of the adoption agency, and with her approval, I was placed in a boarding home in Ottumwa, that specialized in temporary infant care. The agency wanted more physical testing and observation to take place before certifying me as good-to-go. However, in the smudged fine print I read:

> This child was referred for care and observation
> by the Iowa State Division of Child Welfare
> in keeping with the wishes of the mother. As
> is the usual procedure, the Association was to
> board this child for a limited time in order to
> determine suitability for adoption and so that his
> mother might determine whether she wanted to
> permanently release him. He was then moved
> a private boarding home, which is under the
> agency supervision so that he might have care of
> a personal nature.

The actual "Agreement to Surrender" was signed in early June 1949, by Gloria Jean Johnson after I was released by the boarding home. It seems Jean held out until the last minute before deciding to give me away. She never mentioned that when we met. Was she waiting to see if I'd been found suitable for adoption? By then, she was married and pregnant with Charlotte. Would she have kept me, too? That's hard for me to imagine.

The name Meredith Johnson is hand-printed on "Agreement of Adoptive Placement," which my parents co-signed. The adoption agency had earlier stated that my identity would have been withheld from them. That now appeared unlikely, unless they had signed the agreement while my name was shielded from view. Does this mean my parents knew my original name and the identity of my birth mother? I will never know. Reading these documents was confusing, but I could not get over the fact that I was placed in a boarding home for four months, where I was to receive "care of a personal nature." *What does that mean? Who was I with?*

I imagined I had been in the care of several women, each taking a shift during the day and night during those four months. Surely, I was surrounded by well-meaning caretakers, but utterly alone without my real mother. I can only assume from the evidence

I've seen to date that my initial separation from Jean and the lack of a bonding, mirroring connection with any one person in those early months, left an indelible imprint on my psyche. And not just from the "evidence." I know this from the depth of my being.

Through my training in psychotherapy, I've come to understand more about early child development from the works of psychoanalyst John Bowlby. He described the effects of insecure attachment, abandonment, and neglect on the bonding process in early childhood. Separation at birth, compounded by the lack of bonding to a mother figure at this critical moment in a child's development, is a powerful form of emotional trauma—a trauma that can take a lifetime to heal from, if ever. I believe this is true for me. My entire life experience tells me it is so.

I had uncovered vitally important clues in my now unsealed records about who I was, and who I am. I wondered if the isolation in my four-month stay in a boarding home was the cause of my feelings of longing which dated to my early childhood? Even after I was adopted, according to Bowlby's attachment theory, I wouldn't have bonded as deeply with my new mother as I might have if we'd been together from my birth. Was it true? Did that critical window for bonding come and go? Was I already damaged goods? And, of course, my new mother surely may have had her own wounds, which made bonding with me difficult for her. It remains a mystery I will never uncover.

My mother Ruth Rowley loved my three siblings and me with fierce loyalty and unwavering support. But she was not the warm and fuzzy sort. She had her issues, and sometimes her anxiety and occasional outbursts of anger kept us kids at arm's length. I became accustomed to shutting down when she got to be too much for me—too disconnected from something deeper in me that yearned for connection. Although I'm sure she must have loved me, I cannot remember her saying so until later in life. I cannot remember being held closely in her arms, as I must have wanted her to.

She and I were at odds over the years. But there was a teasing tone in how we treated each other, and it took the place of a more traditional mother-son relationship. We shared a respect for each other, but a part of me kept a distance from her. I never thought much about it. I just accepted it. I never questioned my loyalty to her, nor hers to me, but I always felt something between us was missing.

It was through a "Soul Retrieval" session with Michelle McKinney, a shamanic healer in Seattle, that I came to a new understanding of healing from the fragmentation of wounded soul. I sat in a chair in Michelle's office while she offered a few prayers, followed by a rhythmic chant and rattle, after which, as she explains it, her soul silently dove into mine. Her words of explanation were something like this:

> I found a wound in both of you. You both experienced the loss of parent, but at different ages. What I want you to learn, or what perspective is important for you understand now, is that in this life, you were brought here to be her teacher. Your roles were reversed. She was the student, not you. And all those fights you had were more for her benefit than yours. She needed to be brought out of the cocoon of her own troubled past and her small-town ways; and your job was to help her by example—teach her by example. Your rebelliousness was the key. Why do you think you disengaged with her when your brother was born? Your job was to witness her struggle, not to mourn her lack of attention on you. She was very aware of your concern for her when your dad was sick. Even though you lived here in Seattle and she was in Iowa, you were never far from her heart.

Visiting her in her later years was so important
in reassuring her that your bond, and your belief
in her, was unshakeable. That's what a good
teacher does. I left a message for her that your
love for her is still quite alive. Maybe today will
signal a change for you both, as I think there is
some kind of healing or redemption to come. I
can't be sure. It's curious that you told me you
are seeing her in the next month or two for her
100th birthday. Maybe that will be the time for
something to happen.

That was a lot to digest. The idea of a role reversal on a
deeper level of consciousness reminded me of Hillman's reference
to the Myth of Er. I imagined that I had *chosen* this unusual teacher-
student relationship in lieu of a maternal one. Maybe we needed
each other in this way, so we could move beyond the predictable
roles in order to find something important we each needed to
learn. After our session, I felt as if a seed had been planted and I
kept Michelle's message in the back of my mind as something to
explore, like a kōan. Perhaps someday it would make sense to me,
and I let its wisdom seep into my imagination.

Two months after the shamanic session, I flew home
to Burlington for Mom's 100th birthday. My siblings and their
spouses, children, and grandchildren all came together for the
gathering. When I arrived the night before the party, I went
straight to the nursing home and saw my brother David standing
at the doorway to Mom's room. We hugged briefly, and he quickly
turned to her and announced my arrival. "Mom, it's Steve. He just
got here from Seattle." It sounded uncannily like Patty announcing
my arrival at Jean's apartment in Roxbury, Massachusetts.

Ruth was slumped over in her wheel chair. It was nearly
her bedtime, and she looked tired. I could see her frail hands
clutching the thick hospital covers that blanketed her. Her eyes

were half-lidded and her body motionless, so I stepped closer and bent down to tell her I was here now with her.

"Mom, I finally made it. Here I am. You didn't think I was going to miss your birthday party, did you? Somebody's got to eat the frosting."

She shot a look at me, her blue eyes wide open. Her body squirmed a bit so she could sit up. I thought she would respond to me with something mildly clever; but instead, she grabbed both my hands with hers and with a voice that was unnaturally bold and clear, she said simply, "Oh, Steve."

With that, tears erupted and streamed down her nightgown. Her face reddened as her gaze never left mine. She was at full throttle with her throaty cry and heaving torso. A minute went by, and I thought she might calm down, but the quaking of her body only increased. She kept looking at me as though she were trying to send a wordless message that only I would understand. I flashed on my session with Michelle and knew this unforeseen and powerful connection was about that.

Although a hundred-year-old woman was sitting in a wheelchair in front me, I now saw a young woman in her early thirties, holding two-year-old Stevie tightly in her arms, silently praying to be a good mother, frightened to death that she wouldn't be. I held Ruth's hand for fifteen minutes, until her tears were spent. Never before had she cried in my presence. What power she must have had to hold back this much grief for so long, and here I was—her witness, her teacher, her adopted son, and her first child.

She died a year later, not long after her hundred and first birthday. I was not there to say goodbye, but that other-worldly visit we had in the nursing home was as much reunion and farewell as either of us needed, and more than I could have dreamed possible. To have had two mothers was a true blessing in my life, as I needed something different from each.

33. Back to School

When I began taking classes at Pacifica in the fall of 2014, I was literally among school children. Not only was I older than everyone else in my cohort, I was older than all but one of my instructors. I immediately noticed that several of my classmates were unaccustomed to writing academic papers. I wondered how they'd made it through college, let alone into a graduate program. By contrast, I looked forward to writing papers and completing a thesis. The writing assignments were both easy and fun, and I wrote them mostly for myself. Similarly, I dove into the reading assignments with great relish. Reading the works of these psychologists, analysts, and other authors was a privilege and a treat. The school's bookstore was like a candy shop to me. I spent more money on books in those three years than I care to admit. But I kept reading and soaking in more and more, far beyond our class requirements.

The faculty members who were Jungian scholars and analysts deepened my curiosity and passion for depth psychology. But my interests were not limited to Hillman, Campbell, and other well-known pioneers who helped support Pacifica in the beginning. I also began to follow the trails of Zen Buddhism, mythology, neuroscience, somatic therapy, dream tending, Sandplay, and eventually archetypal astrology.

I admit I had second thoughts once I was in the program. I wondered if I had erred in not entering in a training program in Zürich or elsewhere in the US to become a Jungian analyst. But I was suspicious of analyst training, which I believed would be too narrow and orthodox for my blood. Even Jung said, "Thank God, I'm Jung, and not a Jungian."

The Jungian authors whose work was most compelling to me were James Hollis and Thomas Moore. Each spoke and wrote in a manner that was unimpeded by jargon. They had academic chops that were unsurpassed by fellow Jungian scholars, but each had a gift in reaching a broader readership—an audience that sought deeper understanding of themselves and the world around them, untethered from the weight of academic prose. Hollis and Moore remain role models for me as great teachers. I thought it was a shame that little of their work was infused into our curriculum. At times, their natural gifts of communication and insight kept me going, as did the friendships and affection I shared with many classmates and instructors. But I became disaffected with the Counseling Psychology program well before it ended, though I never let anyone know.

What blossomed in its wake was a quasi-personalized program of self-study. I developed a separate reading list and pursued various lines of interest unrelated to Pacifica's curriculum.[18] I freed my mind from the more tedious requirements of the program, and invested my energy in pursuing my more diverse interests. Mentally, I felt free of the constraints of the institution and even the course content. I now was learning on my own terms. I felt as though my entire history, with its many searches and journeys, had brought me to this cherished and exhilarating time in my life. I had struggled for my inner liberation and made my way through it all. I came out of the program as licensed psychotherapist who had simply learned how to be myself. I was sixty-eight years young, with a quarter of my life yet to live. Like Leonard Cohen, I felt like I was kid with a crazy dream, and at long last I was getting started.

34. Finding Him

March 24, 2022 began for me as most mornings do. It was not yet 5:30 and I was half-asleep at my desk, nursing my first cup of coffee, scanning online news on my computer and scrolling through my email. One letter was from 23andMe, to which I'd belonged since its inception in 2007. I had mailed a DNA sample to their Sunnyvale, California, headquarters, hoping to learn all that

I could about my genetic background, including the risk factors for diseases. If I were a ticking time bomb for colon cancer, for example, I wanted to know about it in advance.

And of course, I wanted to identify and possibly meet members of my extended biological family. I had taken hundreds of 23andMe surveys to provide information about my health and background, and I received emails every month or two telling me of new second, third, and fourth cousins. The chance of being related to any of them was close to zero. But despite all the non-starters, I persisted in the remote hope that something new and important might come my way.

Since my reunion with Jean thirty-five years earlier, I held little expectation I would ever discover more than I already knew (which was not much) about my biological father. Through dead-end inquiries with agencies, hundreds of unsuccessful Google searches, and working with psychics, astrologers, and a shaman, I had given up hope of discovering the identity of the other half of my birth parentage.

So, when Wayne Hartley of Austin, Minnesota, contacted me through 23andMe that Thursday morning, sharing DNA evidence that we might as close as first cousins, I jolted awake. Although the family background that he described seemed a garble of confusing information, I emailed him back the scant information I did know about my birth father, and he emailed back that his Aunt Sara, an expert genealogist, would be my best contact now. He warned that she might not respond to me, as a woman in her seventies had recently contacted the family with disquieting news, as she claimed that she was the biological daughter of the male head of the family. But he sent me her email address just the same. My mind was spinning. What had he just told me? *Could it really be?!*

No sooner had I gone for my second cup of coffee than I received an email from Sara. Before I could reply, Wayne wrote back saying that she had already done an Ancestry.com search on me and had added me to their family tree.

Although Wayne had warned me that Sara could be "brash," the tone of her email was matter-of-fact. She wrote that she was my half-sister, and that she had three other sisters—my half-sisters—and that her father was my birth father. Holy shit! I had *four* half-sisters, and these women and I shared the same birth father. Had I really found him at last?!

These revelations washed over me like whitewater roaring through a ruptured dam, flooding my senses, revealing the last piece of the puzzle—the one essential truth of my life that I thought I'd never find. After seventy-three years, I had finally come face-to-face with the man who had fathered me, at least in the imaginal sense. He had long since passed away, but in that moment, he felt quite alive to me.

The photos of him that Sara sent suggested a story of his life before and after me. I now had a clear image of the handsome face I could link with the photos of the young beauty who was my birth mother. I also could compare one of the photos Sara sent with one of me when we were both nineteen, and the resemblance was uncanny. There was no doubt in my mind that I was his biological son, with good looks and athleticism in tow. He was the one.

What also came rushing over me, like someone whose life story flashes by them when they are about to die, were memories from long ago and the many trails my life had taken that led to this moment. The dam had burst at last, and the gates were flooding. In that moment, it washed away any sense of who I thought I was. I felt untethered, floating far above the world I had known.

35. The Coin Lost in the River

No doubt I will discover more clues about my birth father and his family, but even then, his life will remain a mystery to me. Oddly, I don't seem to care as much now. I'm okay with that, although it's a surprise to hear myself say this. Perhaps I've tired of search, but it's more accurate to say I have finally moved on. My insatiable curiosity is now leading me elsewhere.

My experiences with Buddhism, shamanism, depth psychology, and dreaming have conspired to open the shutters of my perception. They have led me to much greater spiritual and psychological awareness. As a young man, the mystery of my adoption weighed heavily upon me. Today, I recognize that it was the intense feelings of yearning and disconnection that propelled me through each stage of my life. I have at last learned to accept the blessings and the pain of being an adoptee, holding both like the energies of yin and yang in circular symmetry.

Like Dorothy in *The Wizard of Oz*, I had to travel to faraway places to return to where I needed to be all along: to my home and to my soul. When I see Charles at our next high school reunion (if we should both live so long), I will tell him: "Yes, I still haven't changed. But I'm also different." The same will be true of him as well. Then I'll chuckle under my breath and disappear before he can recall who I am today or who I was in 1987.

While writing this book, a particular Zen kōan was present for me: *The coin lost in the river is found in the river.* It reminded me of the many mysteries of my life. *Who am I? To what extent did simple twists of fate shape the contours of my destiny?* Over many months, I came to understand firsthand that the purpose of a kōan is to tease the mind while pushing it beyond the limitations of reason and explanation. I came to accept that the teasing of my mind with my haunting questions was akin to opening nested Matryoshka dolls, one after another. Opening one doll or question revealed another in the waiting. The irony of the Martyroska doll analogy is not lost on me, as the traditional Russian dolls represent the mother carrying the family legacy through the child in her womb.

The coin lost in the river is found in the river. The meaning of life, if there is one, may be like a coin that is lost in clear river water. But due to the distortion and refraction of light, it may not be where we think it should be. And searching in the murky waters of life, it may be nearly impossible to discern. Sometimes all we can do is to fumble blindly in the dark.

Like all kōans, my story is incomplete and it has an uncertain ending. After riding the ups and the downs, the joys and challenges of the chapters of my life, I've lost my fondness for certainty. It inhibits curiosity and dampens the capacity to hold the mystery of it all. If there is any meaning to be found in life, I believe it's in the *searching*, not in the *finding*.

Sometimes I think that after all these years, I have found myself. At other times, I'm less sure. I do know one thing, though. I have always been a lucky boy. But I still don't know why. I am more content that way, not knowing. What would life be anyway, without its mysteries slipping through our fingers, like coins in a river—lost and found—again and again?

AFTERWORD

You are not too old and it is not too late
to dive into your increasing depth
where life calmly gives out its own secrets.
~ Rainer Maria Rilke ~

The number of known adoptees in the United States is between 1.5 million and 7 million. I suspect this striking descrepancy is due to the many unique caregiver arrangements that are not recorded as formal adoptions. Examples include relatives who raise a child when the parents are unable or unwilling to, or when someone posing as the natural parent is actually an older sister, a grandmother, a friend of the family, or a sperm donor. In some instances, a caregiver or guardian may assume the identity of the real parent to protect a child, who might otherwise be vulnerable to harm if left in the custody of the natural parent. In other instances, a child may be abandoned and left as a ward of the state or in foster care, often due to physical or mental handicaps or abject poverty. Historically, the most egregious examples of children being taken from the natural parent include slavery and placement in American Indian boarding schools.[19] In such instances, not only is the separation from the mother, family, or tribe traumatizing, but the new reality for children can be exploitive, abusive, and even lethal. Sadly, the list goes on.

There is little commonality of personality or life pattern among adoptees. We are a diverse, yet invisible community. We live in plain sight, but our adopted status is usually unseen by others. It is my belief, however, that adoptees share a fundamental core experience of separation—imprinted in our unconscious minds and held there to defend against the trauma of its memory. This separation of a child from the mother or primary caregiver can leave a deep psychic wound, regardless of the new life and new parents the child may subsequently inherit.

The powerful effects of this type of developmental trauma can last a lifetime. As Kalsched wrote, "But when trauma strikes the developing psyche of a child, a dissociation or split occurs in which the vital core of the self (often represented as a 'child') retreats into the unconscious where it continues to live in 'suspended animation' under a spell cast by the powers of the psyche's survival system."[20]

One powerful remedy for breaking this spell is specialized healing from trauma in psychotherapy or psychoanalysis. But other breakthroughs are achieved through experiences mentioned earlier, such as dreamwork and shamanistic healing. Newer forms of therapy and healing are now being used to treat trauma, which include neurotherapy, somatic therapy, and guided psychedelic and plant medicine experiences.[21]

We adoptees are not the only people who have experienced early childhood trauma. The varieties of wounds a child may experience are countless. But adoptees, having been separated from our biological mothers, nearly always suffer trauma, no matter how well we fare later in life. Imaginally, there is an orphan who lives within us. In depth psychological terms, that orphan is archetypal—universal, with its many faces, names, and energies. The orphan is homeless, restless, disconnected, and in search for something or someone it cannot find, including its very soul. Yet no orphan is beyond redemption. The lost orphan can be found in the shadows and brought to the safety and security of light. Disconnection can be healed by loving reconnection.

For some, the orphan's faint but persistent presence may arise intermittently through feelings and behavior at any stage of life or circumstance. If we are lucky, it can serve as a guide or an ally. Like any unseen aspects of ourselves, if we deny its presence, it can haunt us. As attributed to Jung: "What is not brought to consciousness, comes to us as fate." Whether inflicted by separation at birth or at another time, the challenge is to distinguish the *impact* of the trauma from our *response* to it. It is a cliché, but true nevertheless: Life is what you make of it. We need not live as permanent victims of trauma.

At different times in my life, I've felt like a victim, a survivor, or a hero. These identities, accompanied by the pains, joys, and mysteries of life, have helped define who I am. As I've learned, however, the greater summons is to realize we are more than the many roles we have played over a lifetime. As we strive to understand ourselves beyond the scripts of our daily lives, we may one day discover the deeper essence of ourselves, the very substance of soul.

The process of writing this memoir unearthed truths that had been buried within me; and in that spirit, I wrote this book for myself alone. I quickly discovered that my work had become a private journey of discovery and not simply a recitation of the past. Yet all the while I had the uncanny sense that my ancestors were present, imploring me to make meaning of it all—for my sake, their sake, and the benefit of others. The stories I've shared are particular to my life, but I believe they are universal as well. It is my hope that whatever light this book may cast will illuminate a pathway for others, especially for those who struggle with adoption, identity, and the larger mysteries of life.

I could not have written this memoir at an earlier age. I am grateful that I waited for the right time of my life to tell my story. Now in my seventies, I better appreciate Jung's compelling assertion in the prologue to his memoir *Memories, Dreams, and Reflections*: "Thus, it is that I have now undertaken, in my eighty-third year, to tell my personal myth. I can only make direct statements, only 'tell stories.' Whether these stories are 'true' is not the problem. The only question is whether what I tell is *my* fable, *my* truth."[22] Inspired by Jung, I hope I have honored the gift of my journey by telling *my* truth, and sharing it with you.

The moon and sun are travelers of a hundred generations.
The years, coming and going, are wanderers too.
Spending a lifetime adrift on boat decks,
greeting old age while holding a horse by the mouth—
for such a person, each day is a journey,
and the journey itself becomes a home.
~ Basho, Japanese haiku poet ~

ACKNOWLEDGMENTS

I extend my heartfelt gratitude to my wife, Johanna Caslander, for her love and devotion, and for supporting me during my prolonged but necessary insularity while writing this book, and also to our son, Edward Rowley, for allowing me to bring their lives into this project. Nothing in my memoir and my life works without them.

I am eternally grateful to Robert Galloway, "Mr. G," my lifelong mentor and friend. Bob was the singular impetus for my interest in writing and literature. I also deeply value my experiences with Natalie Goldberg in several of her retreats in New Mexico and France, which helped rekindle my love of the process of writing, especially memoir. I am similarly indebted to Mary Karr. Although we have never met, her masterpiece *The Art of Memoir* has been an unfailing guide for me.

I will forever appreciate the masterful editing and guidance by Arnie Kotler and his invaluable contribution to this book. Jennifer Selig also was enormously encouraging to me from the start. I was lucky to have both Arnie and Jennifer in my corner with our mutual backgrounds in Buddhism (Arnie) and depth psychology (Jennifer).

I was blessed by the skill and insight of the following individuals in helping me better understand my life from an astrological perspective: Laurence Hillman, Lynn Bell, Safron Rossi, and Dennis Flaherty. I also offer my appreciation to many others for their behind-the-scenes support and encouragement including: Pamela Jensen, Darla Dench, Armand Speca, and Tokuden Shinki, Mark Lancaster (Generous Heart Sangha).

As I have utilized a depth psychological perspective throughout this book, I want to single out Jungian analyst and author Donald Kalsched for the brilliant insight expressed throughout his teaching and writing to illuminate the dynamics and impact of trauma on the soul. His personal encouragement and scholarly works have been enormously influential on my writing and my practice as a psychotherapist.

Finally, it is with my deepest gratitude for my parents, Robert Ditto Rowley and Ruth Nelson Rowley, for "picking me from the litter" and loving me from the start. Their steadfast support provided me with a foundation for a life that few enjoy. In a different way, my birth parents provided something unique in and for me that goes beyond our DNA bond. What role I played in your lives, I cannot say. As for me, there is a quality of kinship with you that will be with me always, as it was in the beginning. Thank you both.

PERMISSIONS

ABOUT THE AUTHOR

Photo by Brooke Krog

Stephen Rowley, Ph.D., is a psychotherapist practicing in Bainbridge Island, Washington. His professional past includes serving as an elementary school teacher and principal, and a school district superintendent in Washington and California. He also has been a college professor at three universities in the Pacific Northwest, teaching courses in educational administration and organizational theory and supervising prospective principals and superintendents. He holds a Ph.D. in Administration and Policy Analysis from the Graduate School of Education, Stanford University. He also earned an M.A. in Counseling Psychology (with an emphasis on clinical and depth psychology) from Pacifica Graduate Institute, Santa Barbara, California.

ENDNOTES

1 Haley, Alex. "Resources. Race & American Memory." Grace Farms Foundation. https://gracefarms.org/blog-post/resources-race-american-memory/. February 15, 2017.

2 Chodron, Pema. "In Life by Pema Chodron." PaperMiles Word Press. https://papermiles.wordpress.com/2013/05/21/in-life-by-pema-chordon/. May 21, 2013.

3 Lord, Sterling. *Lord of Publishing: A Memoir.* Lord Publishing Company, 2013, p. 18.

4 Hollis, James. *Hauntings: Dispelling the Ghosts Who Run Our Lives.* Chiron Publications, 2013, p. 53.

5 Kalsched, Donald. *Trauma and the Soul: A Psycho-Spiritual Approach to Human Development and Its Interpretation.* Routledge, 2013, p. 11.

6 Wilhelm, Richard. *The I Ching or Book of Changes.* Bollingen Series XIX, Princeton University Press, 1955, p. xxiv.

7 March, James. "Passion and Discipline: Don Quixote's Lessons for Leadership." YouTube, April 11, 2004, https://www.youtube.com/watch?v=NYmbiv_cbn8&ab_channel=StanfordGraduateSchoolofBusiness.

8 Carrère, Emmanuel. "I'm Happy My Mother's Alive." *97,196 Words: Essays* (see https://academic.macmillan.com/academictrade/9781250758095/97196words) Translated by John Lambert. Farrar, Strauss and Giroux, 2019, p.5.

9 Punnett, Audrey. *The Orphan: A Journey to Wholeness.* Fisher King Press, 2014, p. 141.

10 Rowley, Stephen. "School Closure in Seattle: A Case Study of Educational Decisionmaking." Doctoral dissertation, 1984, https://www.proquest.com/openview/35b9c042bbda3bdc13f1c969249fbf98/1?pq-origsite=gscholar&cbl=18750&diss=y.

11 Whyte, David. *Consolations: The Solace and Underlying Meaning of Everyday Words.* Canongate Books Ltd., 2019, p. 171.

12 Adyashanti. *Falling Into Grace: Insights on the End of Suffering.* Sounds True, 2011.

13 Hillman, James. *The Soul's Code: In Search of Character and Calling.* Grand Central Publishing, 1996, p. 8

14 Hillman, *The Soul's Code,* p. 8.

[15] Campbell, Joseph. *Hermes, Alchemy, & the Voyage of Ulysses*. Collected Works, Audio: Lecture II.2.2.

[16] James, William. Quoted in Paul Lee, *The Quality of Mercy*. Plantonic Academy Press, 1993, p. 12.

[17] Suzuki, Shunryū. *Zen Mind, Beginners Mind*. Shambhala. Weatherhill, 1999, p. 21.

[18] In fairness to the curriculum and instructors of the Counseling Psychology program (MA) of Pacifica Graduate Institute, nearly all course content is mandated by the state of California and accreditation associations. The exception is the robust depth psychology strand of courses in the curriculum, which is unique to Pacifica, and was the reason I chose this school and its program in preparation to become a psychotherapist.

[19] The Indian Child Welfare Act (1978) prevented non-Native officials from removing children from their homes and recognized tribal sovereignty in such circumstanes. This important federal legislation is now under attack. See Forsman, Leonard. "Indian Child Welfare Act is needed to protect Native American children from a return to the Dark Ages." *Seattle Times*, November 25, 2022.

[20] Kalsched, Donald. In program forward to "Healing Trauma: The Lost and Recovered Soul-Child in Depth Psychotherapy: The Jung Memorial Workshop." Washington, D.C., 2018. https://www.jung.org/event-2811873.

[21] Pollan, Michael. *How to Change Your Mind: What the New Science of Psychedelics Teaches Us About Consciousness, Dying, Addiction, Depression, and Transcendence*. Penguin Press, 2018.

[22] Jung, Carl. *Memories, Dreams, Reflections*. Vintage Books Edition, 1989, p. 3.

Printed in the USA
CPSIA information can be obtained
at www.ICGtesting.com
LVHW091702300923
759722LV00002B/339